I AM:

A Biography of Jesus of Nazareth

J. Kie Bowman

Auxano
PRESS

Auxano Press

Tigerville, South Carolina

Copyright © 2014 by Ken Hemphill
All rights reserved.
Printed in the United States of America

ISBN 978-1497461888

Published by Auxano Press

Tigerville, South Carolina

www.AuxanoPress.com

Dedication

Dedicated to my father, the late Van M. Bowman. His last known words were about his Lord, Jesus. He would have loved this book.

Thanks, Dad.

Table Contents

Foreword

The most significant person in history is Jesus Christ. No one else comes close. Name who you will, their influence did not affect humanity as comprehensively as did Jesus.

It might seem strange that someone such as Jesus, born in a stable, reared in a blue-collar family in a remote village, could exert the historical sway He has. Yet that is precisely how God operates. He takes what is seemingly insignificant and does extraordinary works so He receives all the glory.

My longtime friend and fellow pastor, Kie Bowman, has blessed us through his remarkable insights about Jesus Christ in his new book entitled *I AM.* That phrase, "I AM," is set forth in the Gospel of John repeatedly. It reveals the fact that Jesus is Himself God in the flesh, a distinctively Christian concept. All other world religions focus on the insights of a dead man who taught his followers how to work their way up to God to attain salvation. Christianity, however, teaches the exact opposite. Its founder, Jesus Christ, died an atoning, sacrificial death for the sins of mankind (1 John 2:2) but then rose bodily, victoriously, and eternally from the dead! He offers salvation not through good works but by grace through faith to all who will repent, believe, and call on His name. This book provides a fresh study about the teachings of Jesus, His miracles, including His death and resurrection, and, most importantly, how to experience eternal life in Him.

When Christ was born, the great "I AM" stepped onto this planet through the womb of a virgin. In Jesus Christ,

God became one of us. That's why no one else has affected mankind like Jesus. Get to know Him. Because when you know Jesus, you know God.

Steve Gaines, Ph.D.
Senior Pastor
Bellevue Baptist Church
Memphis, Tennessee
March 2014

Acknowledgements

I want to thank Dr. Ken Hemphill, the president of Auxano Press, for having the vision of producing small group teaching tools in this format. I encourage the reader to look at other excellent titles in this series.

I also want to thank my executive assistant, Becky Shipp, for assisting in the editing of the multiple versions of the manuscript before it was finally shipped to the publisher. She read each chapter, made suggestions, caught my typos, and was an encourager throughout the process. Toni Casteel also read and edited each chapter, looking for areas of grammatical improvement. She works fast, too, and did not seem to be overwhelmed by deadlines! Marita Murphy also reviewed the chapters and added an extra set of eyes to help us get it ready for publication. I am deeply appreciative to each of these dedicated Christian women.

I also want to thank Katherine Drye who designed the cover based on a concept using Rembrandt's famous painting *Face of Jesus*. She does good work and is an asset to our team.

I want to thank the congregation and staff of Hyde Park Baptist and The Quarries Church (one church in two locations) for their encouragement, support, and patience as I wrote this book. It has been a labor of love for me, and I hope it will be a blessing to the people I serve.

Finally, I want to thank my wife, Tina, who has patiently allowed our kitchen table to be transformed into a library every night for the last few months as I have written this book. She is a godly woman whom I have shared my life with now for more than thirty-three years. I am deeply grateful to her for being the person she is, a true follower of Jesus of Nazareth.

Introduction

In a beautiful setting on a private prayer retreat with His disciples, Jesus of Nazareth asked a question we are still mulling two thousand years later. His question was simple and direct. He asked, "Who do you say that I am?" (Mark 8:29). This book is an attempt to answer that question. Of course, in many ways the book is an unfinished project because Jesus of Nazareth is the most written about, talked about, and worshipped man who has ever lived. One of His apostles framed the ongoing discussion about Jesus with a prophetic observation: "Now there are also many other things that Jesus did. Were every one of them to be written, I suppose that the world itself could not contain the books that would be written" (John 21:25).

Since I started writing this book, my private study has started to look like a fulfillment of John's words because I have accumulated numerous books about the life of Christ. They are currently stacked on and around my desk because I have needed to know how other authors handled passages and questions about the incredible life of Christ. As a result of my study of other books on the subject of Jesus, I found numerous points of overlap, and, therefore, I have made no attempt to footnote every thought since so much about Him is, by now, common knowledge and repeated in numerous works. Still, there was often a need to quote a source directly, and I have cited sources when appropriate. In some cases, however, I have remembered quotes or stories that serve as illustrations, which are from a lifetime of hearing sermons, studying, preaching, and keeping personal files. As a result, some of the ideas in this book were difficult to footnote but are by no means original to me. Still, I hope I have given credit where it is due in every case possible.

I hope this volume adds to the conversation about the life and ministry of Jesus in two ways. For one thing, it is written to draw our attention, as believers, back to the gospel and to the man, Jesus, who actually lived, died, and was raised to life in Israel. I hope scenes from His life will engage our thinking and challenge us to go deeper with Him as Lord and see His relevance to our lives in the twenty-first century. I have tried to peer behind the scenes of familiar events to attempt a contemporary reconstruction of the people and places we read about in the Gospels. I have hoped to move the reader back in time to get a feel for the situations in the life of Christ from the perspective of the people who were actually there. At the same time, this is a literary effort for the twenty-first century, and I have tried to write in such a way that the reader is moved to keep reading (without getting bogged down in historical and geographical details, which, I admit, I find interesting and informative).

In any event, the book is written to help believers know more about Jesus Christ so they can know Jesus Christ more! With this in mind, it is written to be taught in small groups for a Bible study curriculum. In this way believers can disciple others.

The second reason for writing this book is for those who aren't convinced or don't know what to think of Jesus. My prayer is that this book will end up in the hands of those who do not currently follow Christ as Lord. I encourage readers to give it as a gift to those who do not know Jesus and allow it to be a place to begin spiritual conversations. The size of the book makes it small enough to be read quickly, and yet it focuses on the events from the life of Jesus that point to His humanity, deity, sacrificial death on the cross, and conquest over death. He is presented here as the Son of God who lived and died and rose again so we can know God.

Whatever else anyone can say about Jesus of Nazareth, one thing is certain—we haven't forgotten Him. As I complete this writing, His image is crowding the national periodicals at check-out lines across the country just in time for Easter. His likeness on the covers perennially helps sell more magazines. Since I started this project, at least two books about Jesus, with drastically different interpretations of His life, have gone to number one on The New York Times Best Sellers List. A movie about the life of Jesus is currently earning millions of dollars at theater box offices and surprising some observers in the process. Jesus once asked His disciples, "Who do men say that I am?" This book is a contribution, from one of His followers, to that ongoing discussion.

J. Kie Bowman
March 2014
Austin, Texas

"What If God Was One of Us?"

Focal Text: John 1:1–14

The hollow, lifeless expressions of an odd cast of characters were even more pronounced because they were shot in sepia tone. The Coney Island boardwalk has usually served as a place of entertainment, but that day it looked more like a bad dream where sad-faced people seemed to be merely going through the motions of living.

The scenes on the boardwalk, which leave the viewer with the impression of watching a bizarre carnival, were from a popular music video that accompanied a top-ten pop song from the 1990s, written quickly to impress a girl. The song "One of Us" went on to receive three Grammy award nominations, including Song of the Year.

The chorus and the theme of the song raise the question, "What if God was one of us?"[1] Not surprisingly, the incarnation is an unexpected subject for the Top 40.

Of course the unusual lyrics might leave some Christians offended, suggesting that God would become a "slob" or that He might be aimlessly riding a bus with no particular sense of direction, but the larger question persists: "What if God was one of us?" What if He came here and lived here and was in some ways indistinguishable from the average people all around Him? The fact that He did just this is the message of the New Testament and one of the many unique distinctions of Christianity. God became one of us. The man He became was a carpenter from an obscure Galilean village in the hills of northern Israel, Jesus of Nazareth.

For two thousand years since the early church, Roman Catholic, Eastern Orthodox, and Protestant teaching has insisted on telling the Christmas story from the Gospels of Matthew and Luke. As a result of that understandable persistence, almost everyone in the Western world can retell at least some of the major points of the birth story of Jesus. The wise men, the virgin Mary, and the "little town of Bethlehem" are all part of our cultural pool of common knowledge.

It is obvious from the biblical Christmas story, especially the impact on Joseph and Mary, that Jesus began to make an impression from conception, even before His birth. The celebration around the world of Christmas today is evidence enough of the fact. Yet, as well known as the birth narrative may be, the biography of Jesus precedes the manger story in Bethlehem. He existed even before the angel overshadowed Mary and she miraculously conceived.

Where was Jesus before that first Christmas? What was He doing before the day in which He voluntarily hid Himself as an embryo in the confines of an Israeli, teenaged virgin's womb?

The Word
John 1:1–3

The last living apostle began his Gospel with a spiritually intriguing, yet almost incomprehensible premise. Without hesitation, the elder statesman bluntly affirmed that Jesus, whom he had known personally, existed with God before the beginning of time. "In the beginning was the Word, and the Word was with God, and the Word was God. He was with God in the beginning" (John 1:1–2, NIV). In some ways this may be the most astounding claim of the New Testament. If God became a man and lived with all of the temptation, suffering, and hardship we all endure, including death, then everything else Jesus did takes on a significance with a gravitational pull great enough to align all of Scripture around the life, teaching, death, resurrection, and continuing ministry of Jesus. For John and other New Testament writers, that is exactly what they believed: Jesus of Nazareth was, in fact, the God of the Old Testament in human form. It means, as the old saying goes, "Jesus is either Lord of all or not Lord at all." For the writers of the New Testament, Jesus was the Lord God (Matt. 1:23; Phil. 2:5–6; Heb. 1:3).

John framed the declaration of faith in his Gospel by introducing Jesus, not as a baby in Bethlehem but with an entirely new designation describing One who has always existed as "the Word." While the term "the Word" can be found in some Greek philosophical writings from the ancient world, such as the fifth-century BC philosopher Heraclitus and the third-century BC Stoics, the apostle John's orientation is completely Jewish and is therefore grounded in the Old Testament. John's use of the term "the Word" is not a philosophical, ethereal force or a universal "soul," as the Greek philosophers used the word. Instead, for John "the Word" is none other than the God the Jewish prophets knew and the Hebrew Scriptures declared. In addition, "the Word" is more than a mystical power or a nebulous spirit; the Word is a person. John makes that clear when he confidently asserts, "The Word became flesh and dwelt among us" (John 1:14). To add further to this mind-boggling truth, John says, "We have seen his glory" (John 1:14). In other words John knew Him! This is more than a philosophical principle. The Word is God who became a man!

The term translates the Greek word *logos*, which means "word" and stems from the verb meaning "to say" or "to speak." John's knowledge of the Old Testament reminded him that the psalmist, hundreds of years earlier, had declared, "By the word of the Lord the heavens were made, their starry host by the breath of his mouth" (Ps. 33:6, NIV). The Word is God's creative power. Other New Testament writers affirmed the same truth. For instance, the writer to the Hebrews reminds us, "By faith we understand that the universe was created by the word of God, so that what is seen was not made out of things that are visible" (Heb. 11:3). The examples in the Old Testament alone of the phrase "the word of God" or, more often, "the word of the Lord" are numerous, occurring more than one hundred times! John's understanding of the concept of "the Word" (like the other New Testament writers) was drenched in Old Testament imagery and teaching.

Along those same lines, just as the Bible is introduced by the phrase, "In the beginning God" (Gen. 1:1), John's Gospel introduces "the Word" in the same way, "In the beginning was the Word" (John 1:1). That remarkable similarity is obviously intentional. The Hebrew title for Genesis is actually the phrase "in the beginning" and suggests another reason John refers to Jesus as "the Word." When we are introduced to God in Genesis, He is the Creator of heaven and earth. His way of creating is to speak things into existence. For instance, everything in the world, from Genesis 1:3–30, including man, is created. At least fourteen times in those verses, the Scripture says "God said" or "God called," and the things came to be. Perhaps the most familiar example is found in the phrase, "And God said, 'Let there be light,' and there was light" (Gen. 1:3). God creates by what He says, by His Word. Not surprisingly, John's second affirmation about "the Word," found in John 1:3, is identical to the truth played out repeatedly in the Genesis creation account. "Through him all things were made; without him nothing was made that has been made" (John 1:3, NIV). Just as God was creating in the beginning, so Jesus was creating in the beginning. Jesus is the Word who created everything, but since He "was with God in the beginning" (John 1:2), He Himself is the uncreated Word. There has never been a time when Jesus did not exist. That is John's glaringly conspicuous point. Jesus of Nazareth is God and He has been forever.

What "the Word" Means for Us
John 1:14

God could have revealed Himself in any number of ways and has (see Heb. 1:1). Through John's Gospel we discover that God chose for Jesus the self-revealing description of "the Word." What does it suggest that God wants us to know Him as "the Word"? At the very least we should assume the God known as "the Word" has something to say! God speaks. He wants to be heard. God is a communicator. Since the Word became flesh, we should understand Him as an extremely personal God who wants to speak to and have fellowship with His creation. He wants to speak with you! Imagine for a moment the implications of that truth. God wants to communicate with you so much that He became one of us in order to get to know us, so that we can, in turn, get to know Him. It's astounding.

When we feel alone, God speaks into the emptiness and says, "I am with you." When we are afraid, God speaks into the darkness with the assurance, "Fear not." When we are uncertain about which way to turn, God speaks into our aimlessness and says, "Follow Me." Everywhere we look in Scripture, we find God communicating. He is always speaking. But in Jesus the invisible Voice becomes a man who not only talks to us but also talks like us!

Jesus, therefore, is God's most intimate communication with us, and because He was a man, God entered into a conversation with His people as never before. Because God lived with us as one of us, the dialogue between God and us has never been more possible or more tangible. In the Old Testament God spoke to the prophets, but in the New Testament Jesus is God's Word to every believer (Heb. 1:1). You can assume, therefore, that He is speaking to you now. Jesus said, "My sheep hear my voice" (John 10:27). Jesus continues to speak to His followers, so developing an "ear to hear" should be a priority for all of us. The obvious key to hearing God, of course, is knowing Jesus, who is introduced to us as "the Word" of God.

We can see that communication with God is important from God's perspective because He became a man and suffered and died in order to reveal Himself fully to us. When I was in college, before the days of cell phones, I frequently called my parents in Alaska, and I always placed a collect call, which meant they paid the long-distance charges. When God wanted to communicate with man, He paid the incredibly high cost to do so by sending His own Son, the eternal Word of God, to die in our place.

We realize, by looking at Jesus, that God is a communicator, but how did "the Word" enter the conversation of human experience, and what does that reveal about Him? Put another way, when "the Word" spoke, what accent did He have?

Jesus of Nazareth was born in what Luke called a "manger" (Luke 2:7), a Greek word used to describe a place where domestic animals were housed, like a stall inside a barn. His parents had only enough money to offer pigeons as a gift in the temple for His dedication (Luke 2:24). The Old Testament provided that option as an alternative for the poor residents who could not afford a lamb (Lev. 12:6–13). He had royal blood, but obviously the royal line of David had fallen on hard times.

He was raised in the small village of Nazareth in the rugged hills of Northern Israel, with a population of perhaps as few as 125 residents. The town is never mentioned in the Old Testament. His parents were poor, working-class Jews, and He followed in the footsteps of Joseph as a local carpenter (Mark 6:3). Once His ministry began, there are references to a residence where He stayed (John 1:39), but there is no indication that He ever owned property or even His own house. His followers were drawn mostly from the poorer population (Mark 12:37). They must have seen Him as one of their own. He was born in a borrowed barn and was buried in a borrowed tomb. In between He was usually the guest of a supporter and seemed to rely primarily on the generosity of others to provide for His needs.

What does all of this say about "the Word"? For one thing it is completely in line with the prophesy of Isaiah who wrote, "For he grew up before him like a young plant, and like a root out of dry ground; he had no form or majesty that we should look at him, and no beauty that we should desire him. He was despised and rejected by men; a man of sorrows, and acquainted with grief; and as one from whom men hide their faces he was despised, and we esteemed him not" (Isa. 53:2–3, ESV). The Word, who appeared as God in the flesh, deliberately arrived wrapped in the anonymous, unsophisticated garb of poverty. At the very least God's presence with humanity's poor and underprivileged working-class suggests that "the Word" speaks the language of man's most common vulnerabilities. He is, after all, as the song suggests, "One of us."

For Memory and Meditation

"In the beginning was the Word, and the Word was with God, and the Word was God. He was in the beginning with God." John 1:1–2

---

[1] Eric M. Bazilian, "One of Us," © Human Boy Music / Warner/ Chappell Music, Inc.

The Real Temptation of Christ
Focal Text: Matthew 4:1–11

Can you see Him there—a man alone in the distance, baked by the sun; His dark, matted hair whipping in the wind, coated with sand and drenched with sweat? His clothes are dirty, caked with the environment blown on and all around Him. They are little more than rags after all these weeks, hanging loose and ill fitting on His bony, sinewy frame. His feet are calloused and toughened from the blisteringly hot desert, as if His skin were turning to dried-up, old cracked leather. His young face is gaunt and tight; His eyes are deep set from starvation; and His cheekbones appear unnaturally high and sharp, riding above His hollowed, bearded cheeks. He walks alone deliberately, day after day through the most inhospitable place He could find. The locals call this unpopulated region *Yeshimon*, which means "desolation." It's an apt description.

Loose, jagged rocks have caused Him to stumble more than once as He makes His way up and down inclines more suited for the scorpions, serpents, and wild, desert goats. The sun is relentless. The precipitous peaks drop off suddenly hundreds of feet into valleys long ignored by everyone except the odd desert nomads and a few antisocial, religious, hermit-like extremists who have cloistered themselves away into a small, monastic outpost studying prophecy and waiting for the end of the world, but they ignore Him.

The twisted stratum of His self-imposed exile is complete in its unforgiving harshness to every living thing and stretches across 425 square miles of scorched earth. The winters here feel like summer everywhere else, and the summers are an intolerable, dry furnace with average temperatures of well over 100 degrees in the infrequent shade that might be found under an overhanging cliff. He has been out here, voluntarily, for almost a month and a half with no food—not a single bite. Water is nearly as scarce as on the surface of Mars except for the shallow, mud-thickened, greenish, silt-filled, mineral-rich, small river—no bigger at this geographical point than a stream winding sluggishly along a narrow, southern path down to the lowest point on earth below sea level.

His entire body has suffered. From the daily weight loss and the permanent hardness of every place he has stopped for rest, to the constant discomfort of the endless heat, it has all been a daily part of the decision to seek the solitude of the desert.

No one in his right mind would wander that unpeopled wasteland any longer than he was forced to. And yet there He is. The suffering began within moments of climbing those lifeless, quiet, rocky slopes that find their base near a massive body of stagnate, glassy, salt water where nothing lives. At times the silence has been punctured only by the sound of His own exhausted breathing but never by even the faintest sound of another human voice.

The days have been long and strenuous. The nights are even worse. Comfort has been forgotten and at times must seem as distant as if it had never really existed. Other men have lost their way, their sanity, and their lives in this endless wasteland of yellowish-brown, baked limestone. He won't last much longer like this; He has almost reached the physical point of no return.

What is He doing here? Is He looking for something? Is He hiding from someone? Why did He surrender His young life to this almost unbearable isolation?

Look. He's coming closer. His dark eyes are flashing with the penetrating look of another world. He is like no one else you've ever seen. Yet you realize you know Him.

It's Jesus of Nazareth.

The God of the Desert

If you could have been an eyewitness to the events in the Judean wilderness two thousand years ago, the scene imagined above would be close to reality. Three of the four Gospels mention it. So, why did Jesus spend forty days alone in the Judean desert? He had been mostly obscure and essentially unnoticed for the first thirty years of His life, so we might find it unusual that He began His public ministry out of the watchful eye of the public. In an age of social media, when many of us have "followers" and post blogs, pictures, and daily updates about often mundane events, the most profoundly important person who ever lived chose a path of less notice in order to have more significance.

Jesus wasn't the first man or movement to find God's purpose in the desert. Centuries earlier Abraham gravitated "toward the Negev," the southern desert of Israel (Gen. 12:9; 13:1–4). Later Moses encountered God for the first time in the flames of an inextinguishable, burning bush in the Midian Desert in modern northwestern Arabia (Exod. 3:1–6). When the people of Israel left Egypt, they spent four decades in the desert learning the hard way about unfaith-fulness to the God who keeps His word (Josh. 5:6). Later King David escaped the threat of death during a military coup by hiding in the same desert where Jesus would fast for forty days. While there David saw the obvious parallels between the chalky desert floor and a spiritually dry soul in need of God (Ps. 63:1–4).

Of all the men who preceded Jesus into God's "school of the desert," perhaps the most remarkable was His con-temporary: John the Baptist. He flourished in the desert and apparently lived his entire life there, where he experienced an almost unequaled spiritual depth (Luke 1:80).

Likewise Paul apparently learned the secrets of God in the desert. After his conversion in Damascus, Syria, the apostle "disappeared" into the Arabian Desert. No one knows why, but John R. W. Stott, reflecting on Paul's own testimony (Gal. 1:16–18), said the desert was for "quiet and solitude" where "he had Jesus to himself as it were, for three years of solitude in the wilderness."[1]

Therefore, we might draw the conclusion that when God wanted a "father figure" of faith, a nation of followers, a lawgiver leader, a man after His own heart, a forerunner for His Son, and a trailblazing missionary, He "made" them all in the desert. He built them where the human heart can seek God in solitude and secret. In each case the time in the desert was preparation for something else.

Apparently when God has a great plan for us that, in turn, affects others in the body of Christ, He takes us to a "school of the desert" where He, Himself, is both the subject and the Teacher! When He wants to prepare us for "what's next" in the kingdom, He leads us to a "personal desert" where distractions and other interests are set aside and our focus is Him. That is partly the reason Jesus went there. But how could the Son of God need additional "preparation"?

The New Testament presents Jesus this way: as much God as if He weren't man and as much man as if He weren't God! Hebrews 5:8 reminds us, "Although he was a son, he learned obedience from what he suffered." Jesus did not need to unlearn any bad habits like we do, but in order to relate to our situation, He experienced—that is He "learned"—what doing God's will means in the face of brutal difficulties! In this way the forty days in the desert prepared Him for what He would face during the three years of His public ministry, which finally led to the cross. When we enter those seasons of desert training and God strips away our distractions and securities in order to prepare us for what comes next, we can be assured Jesus relates to everything we are going through. He went through it Himself!

Spiritual Warfare in the Desert
Matthew 4:4–10

Since Jesus went to the desert to receive preparation for His future ministry and since He is the ultimate role model for us, what do we learn from His experience about the best ways to benefit from those preparation seasons of life? The lessons are spiritual and reproducible in our lives.

Jesus fasted. Shouldn't we? What is fasting, and why did Jesus do it? Ron Dunn once said, "Fasting detaches us from earth and prayer attaches us to heaven."[2] Throughout Scripture godly men sought God through fasting and prayer. Moses, Elijah, and Daniel are prime Old Testament examples (Exod. 34:28–29; 1 Kings 19:7–8; Dan.10:2–3) of men who fasted and prayed before experiencing significant spiritual victories. Jesus taught His followers to fast and pray as regular expressions of devotion to God (Matt. 6:5–18). But why?

Those who have practiced the discipline of fasting regularly report such spiritual benefits as intensified mental and spiritual focus during prayer. Moses retreated for prayer and fasting before receiving the Ten Commandments. Daniel fasted when he was burdened about understanding a prophetic vision. Ezra called an urgent public fast to seek God's protection, and Joel called a nation to fast during a season of national repentance (Ezra 8:21–23; Joel 2:12). Each of these instances highlights the sense of urgency and spiritual intensity associated with fasting. When joined with prayer, fasting alerts our spiritual awareness and calls our attention to focus on the things of God.

Clearly Jesus used the spiritual discipline of fasting to its maximum potential when He engaged in spiritual combat with the devil in the wilderness (Matt. 4:1–3). But fasting is more than abstaining from food. While Matthew doesn't specifically mention the prayer life of Jesus during the wilderness temptation, it is reasonable to assume it is understood since fasting is almost universally associated with prayer in Scripture. It is also possible to imagine Jesus spending virtually the entire forty days in prayer. After all, He taught His disciples to pray continuously and not to give up (Luke 18:1). The eighteen times we find Jesus in prayer in the New Testament reveal a life wholly devoted to prayer. No one who knows the life of Jesus should hesitate in seeing the temptation experience as a long, personal prayer retreat, which is exactly what it was. Since Jesus faced the tempter by fasting and prayer, His followers should as well.

Jesus also had a weapon at His side perfectly suited for spiritual warfare. He was armed with the Word of God. Three times the tempter offered Jesus an opportunity to sin, and three times Jesus overcame the temptation with Scripture (Matt. 4:3–10).

The devil suggested that Jesus should give in to His natural appetites and satisfy His hunger, that He should sensationalize His ministry with a public swan dive off the highest point of the temple, and that He should commit the ultimate betrayal by worshipping Satan in return for personal gain (vv. 4:3–9). Each time Jesus refused directly and simply by quoting Scripture (vv. 4: 4, 7, 10).

Each time Jesus confronted the devil in the desert, He quoted from the book of Deuteronomy. I have often wondered if perhaps Jesus had tucked the scroll of Deuteronomy into a bag for His retreat into the wilderness. Of course, a compelling case can be made that Jesus, as a devoted, young Jewish man, had long since memorized the words of Scripture. As the psalmist declared centuries earlier, "I have hidden your word in my heart that I might not sin against you" (Ps. 119:11, NIV). No doubt Jesus, the living Word of God (John 1:1–2, 14), had no trouble memorizing the Word He Himself inspired! Still it is a beautiful thought to imagine Jesus alone in the desert, prayerfully fasting, and spending hours, day after day, pouring over the Scripture!

In any event we are left with this portrait of our Lord modeling for all of us how to face the tempter, overcome temptation, and win the battles of spiritual warfare. First, He was moved and led by the Holy Spirit (4:1). Next Jesus recognized the value of prayer and fasting alone with God.

Finally, Jesus used Scripture like a weapon against the enemy.

When Christians today are called to a desert of spiritual preparation, when we are tempted by the enemy of our souls, we will want to follow our Lord's example. Seek the fullness of the Holy Spirit. Give yourself to a life of prayer and fasting. Memorize, turn to, and trust the Bible. When we exercise these disciplines, we will be able to beat the devil when we meet him!

For Memory and Meditation

"But he answered, 'It is written, "Man shall not live by bread alone, but by every word that comes from the mouth of God."'" Matthew 4:4

---

[1] John R. W. Stott, *The Message of Galatians* (Leicester, England: Inter-Varsity Press, 1968), 34.

[2] @RevRonDunn, Twitter post on September 19, 2013, 6:32a.m., http://twitter.com/RevRonDunn.

The Worst Response to the Best Sermon

Focal Text: Luke 4:14–30

History has a way of forgetting most sermons, along with the preachers who delivered them. In nearly every generation, however, a few preachers stand out from their peers, and their legacies and books linger in minds and on library shelves of future generations. G. Campbell Morgan was one of those men.

On two separate occasions he served as pastor of the prestigious Westminster Chapel, just a block from Buckingham Palace, and was known throughout the British Empire and across the United States as one of the most prolific evangelical Bible teachers and authors of his era. His friendships with nineteenth-century preachers Charles Spurgeon and D. L. Moody and his ministry lasting well into the twentieth century make him an important and pivotal figure in the development of modern evangelicalism. But He didn't start out that way.

As a child Morgan was tutored at home and never had formal theological training. The first time he applied for ordination he was turned down for an apparent lack of ministerial aptitude; the ordination council thought he couldn't preach! Feeling dejected, he boarded a train for home but not before sending a one-word telegram to his father. All it said was, "Rejected." His father promptly sent back the best possible reply: "Rejected on earth—accepted in heaven!"

Congregations sometimes get it wrong. The ordination council got it wrong with G. Campbell Morgan. But no

21

congregation ever missed it as badly as the one in Nazareth the day Jesus came home to preach.

The Hometown of Jesus
Luke 4:16–22

Jesus knew the men who attended the synagogue in Nazareth, and they knew Him. They could be narrow-minded, suspicious of new ideas, reactive, and potentially explosive. They were all those things and more the day a "hometown boy" preached in their small synagogue.

Jesus must have known what their reaction would be. He and His family had attended that same fellowship for years. He had patiently listened to their biases, their prejudices, their cliquishness; and He had taken note of their angry rhetoric at various times. They were accustomed to being ignored as a town because they were small and no one of importance or influence came or went from Nazareth. It was a town on the way to nowhere; the main roads all ran in other directions. For some of the small-town power brokers, the "big fish in the little pond" types, keeping Nazareth the way it was worked just fine. If you crossed them, they might just take you to a bluff on the edge of town and throw you to your death. That's exactly what they tried to do with Jesus.

Daily life in Nazareth was never easy. It could be brutal. Perhaps the difficulty of life there contributed to the severe mind-set of the residents. The town was isolated and unnoticed by the surrounding villages. Unlike the towns around the Sea of Galilee that supported the fishing industry or the commercial, political, and religious activity that drew people to Jerusalem, Nazareth could barely support its own small, struggling population.

For one thing its water supply was limited to the unusual amount of rain from October until March that kept the streets muddy most of the winter. The lack of a large natural body of water—Nazareth had no lakes or rivers—kept the population small and the economy depressed. A family of tradesmen, like the family of Joseph of Nazareth, could make a living with building tools—constructing houses and doing household repairs for the neighbors. They were carpenters who worked with wood, stone, and even metal. If a job involved building materials, repairs, or new construction of any kind, they were the family to call. If the synagogue needed a new roof or new door hinges, or if the frequent winds common in the area caused damage of any kind, Joseph and his sons could be trusted to do the job right. Life for the people of the ancient town of Nazareth was austere, impoverished, and essentially unchanged by anything the outside world had to deal with.

The welcome break from the dreary, windy, wet, winter days and the long, hot, dusty, summers came each week as the religious town celebrated the Sabbath. The houses were pressed so close together that everyone was keenly aware of everyone else's lives. Their lives revolved around family, work, and faithfulness to their Jewish faith. Little changed in Nazareth except that each year older citizens died and a few babies were born. Otherwise the observance of Jewish tradition, laws, and customs kept the local people from going stir crazy from the monotony and the strenuous but unprofitable workload. Most of the citizens would have it no other way. They adjusted to their poverty and accepted what they saw as the stern and unbending will of God.

People liked Jesus as He grew up. He didn't cause trouble like other restless boys, and He had a confident but quiet respect for older people. He did what His parents expected, and He was a regular at the synagogue services with an aptitude for the Torah even from His childhood. The scandal surrounding His birth was never completely forgotten, but His family, in time, had been accepted. They were godly people.

Joseph rarely said much, and Mary could be found helping others wherever she could. In the synagogue services the depth of this family became obvious. They were faithful, and the breadth of Jesus' knowledge of Scripture reminded the older residents of His mother, Mary, when she was a child. So when word began to circulate that Jesus was teaching and even performing miracles, the religious people of Nazareth, grudgingly aware of their low status on the nation's cultural ladder, were only too eager to claim Him as their own. That first Sabbath back in Nazareth, the other men in the synagogue never took their eyes off of Him. He was a celebrity from their town. Nothing like this had ever happened in Nazareth before.

Given His family's long standing in the village; the fact that His mother, sisters, brothers, and presumably their own young families still lived in Nazareth; and the popularity of Jesus Himself, what happened that day? What did Jesus say during that worship service that could have caused tempers to flare to the point they were willing to murder one of their favorite sons in a violent mob action?

The Sermon
Luke 4:18–27

If there was an abundance of anything in Nazareth, it was rock. As a result, the stone and mud houses all looked alike, and the synagogue was not much different. As Jesus stepped into the intentionally drab, dimly lit house of worship, it was familiar territory. He had attended there faithfully with Joseph and His brothers every Sabbath day virtually all of His life, but this would be the last time.

Luke's description of what transpired that day not only focuses on the inaugural sermon of Jesus; it also provides the first glimpse from antiquity of an actual synagogue worship service. The order was remarkably similar in every city. The large Torah scroll was handled as one the most precious and perhaps expensive items in the village. The men sang from the Psalms with a melodic depth known only to an oppressed people who find an escape for their souls through their songs. They read from the Law of Moses in Hebrew, and either the reader or someone else would translate the Hebrew into the more common Aramaic spoken by the Jews of Jesus' time. They prayed and asked God to deliver them from the hands of their Gentile oppressors in Rome. Then a reading from the Prophets and a sermon on the Scripture followed. There was no "pastor" as we envision the role. Instead, lay leaders chose a "ruler of the synagogue," who in turn chose the volunteer reader and preacher for the day.

When they handed Jesus the scroll of Isaiah, He deliberately turned to a beautiful passage promising a future Messianic Age when God's Anointed Servant would shepherd the troubled and wounded souls in Israel. The sermon that followed was unlike any they had ever heard before.

"The Spirit of the Lord is upon me, because he has anointed me to proclaim good news to the poor. He has sent me to proclaim liberty to the captives and recovering of sight to the blind, to set at liberty those who are oppressed, to proclaim the year of the Lord's favor" (Luke 4:18–19).

The people loved the Scripture, and the choice of that passage was especially encouraging. It was a perfect selection for their local hero to read. Jesus sat down, a signal He was ready to preach, and the attention of every person was riveted on Him.

He boldly proclaimed that the seven-hundred-year-old prophecy of Isaiah was being fulfilled in their lifetime. Jesus said, "Today this Scripture has been fulfilled in your hearing" (v. 21). But He didn't stop there. The more He spoke, the more the emotional temperature of the room heated up and became volatile.

Jesus chided them for wanting miracles like the ones they heard He had done in other places. He insisted that He was an unwelcome prophet in His own hometown. They must have been listening in disbelief. What was He talking about? No one had said anything of the sort. Was He reading their body language or their minds? Or did Jesus have nearly thirty years of firsthand knowledge of the smallness of these provincial, shortsighted traditionalists?

Then Jesus crossed the line. He reminded them that during the prophet Elijah's time, while Jews everywhere in the Holy Land were suffering from a multiyear drought, God sent the prophet only to the house of a Gentile woman. The men listening to Jesus were looking at one another and at Him as if they could not believe their own ears. No doubt the sound of the small congregation, perhaps fifty to seventy-five men, was made more indistinct as each man began verbally grumbling their displeasure. But before the synagogue ruler or one of the elderly men could speak up to dispute with Jesus, He added insult to injury by bringing up another example from Scripture. Elisha, He reminded them, had also ignored every Israelite suffering from leprosy but healed a Syrian instead—another Gentile.

The sermon was over at that point. Church was dismissed without a benediction. The crowd that loved having a well-known preacher from their village forced Him to the edge of a precipice at the outskirts of town where they had every intention, in the blind rage of the moment, of killing Him. Without explanatory details Luke tells us Jesus merely slipped away unnoticed. He never returned.

What Does It All Mean?
Luke 4:18–30

What do we learn about Jesus from the incident at Nazareth? For one thing, Jesus of Nazareth was no passive mystical guru. Instead, Jesus was confrontational, fearless, and robust.

Beyond a study of His personal characteristics, the section of Scripture He chose that day is revealing on multiple levels. He clearly saw Himself as the Spirit-anointed fulfillment of messianic prophecy. The words *Messiah* in Hebrew and *Christ* in Greek both mean "the anointed one." From the beginning of His ministry, Jesus knew who He was and what He was sent to do.

Along those same lines, Jesus was dependent from the beginning on the Holy Spirit. That feature of His life and ministry would also factor favorably on the impact His followers made on the first-century world as Luke would later demonstrate in the book of Acts. In other words, since Jesus was Spirit-filled, anointed, and dependent, all of us should follow His example.

The focus of our Lord's message, the theme that would form the contours of His ministry, is also clear from His choice of Scripture that day. He would spend His time ministering to the poor, the imprisoned, the blind, and the oppressed (vv. 18–19). He would be the Savior of the forgotten man, the beaten, and the sick. He came intentionally attracted to weakness. His people would be the same ones most other people overlook.

But what about any of that would incite a group of neighbors to become a gang of killers? It was the insistence of Jesus that God wanted to reach the Gentiles, even to the exclusion of Jews at times, that lit the flames of their zealous nationalism and hatred.

Jesus introduced a new way of thinking about God. The prophets had hinted at God's acceptance of the Gentile nations. But Jesus placed the issue front and center as the cornerstone of His ministry: God loves the Gentiles, too! This was an entirely new and unacceptable concept for the men of Nazareth even though the Old Testament had alluded to it since the origins of the Jewish people. God had promised Abraham, the Father of the Jewish people, he would be a blessing to the Gentiles, "And in your offspring shall all the nations of the earth be blessed, because you have obeyed my voice" (Gen. 22:18).

The Jews had resisted the message of blessing the Gentiles, but that was all about to change. Jesus was so insistent on that subject He was willing to die for it. Three years later on a cross in Jerusalem, that's exactly what He did. From the beginning of His ministry, Jesus made clear He had come to reach the entire world and deliver a message of salvation. As His followers we should be willing to do the same in our world.

For Memory and Meditation
"The Spirit of the Lord is upon me, because he has anointed me to proclaim good news to the poor." Luke 4:18a

Man of Prayer

Focal Text: Mark 1:21–39

Does prayer make any difference? If so, how do we know? That's what Mario Beauregard, neuroscientist from the University of Montreal's Neuroscience Research Center, wanted to examine. He wondered if the "materialists" in his academic circles were correct. They have generally concluded the great religious leaders of history merely suffered from frontal-lobe epilepsy, which contributed to an artificial mystic sense of a divine presence. Dr. Beauregard speculated that he could disprove that theory using the science of neuroimaging.[1]

To do it he needed to find a test group of praying people. Near one of the busiest rapid-transit systems in Canada, the researcher found the group he needed. Nestled behind protective stone walls in the clanging industrial area of Montreal, the quiet nuns of the Carmelite Order live to pray. It is their life's work. For example, the fifteen nuns studied by the neuroscientist had logged a combined 210,000 hours in silent, contemplative prayer by their average age of fifty.[2]

Dr. Beauregard knew functional magnetic resonance imaging (fMRI) could "map" the brain activity of the nuns when they were in a state of deep, contemplative prayer. What he discovered was incredible.

The materialists in the academic field of neuroscience discount religious experience as mere emotion stimulated in the temporal lobes. When these sensations of well-being occur, the materialists argue that the praying person confuses that positive feeling for a connection with God. If that is the case, then it should be possible to prove or disprove it with neuroimaging. If during intense times of prayer the temporal lobes are active while the rest of the brain is fairly inactive, then perhaps the materialists are correct. In that case the sense of connection to God is just emotion, and "God" would be merely a function of the human brain.

The nuns' fMRI during prayer showed something different. Instead of finding activity only in the temporal lobes, the research team found significant activity in multiple areas of their brains occurring simultaneously, including in the "right medial orbitofrontal cortex, right middle temporal cortex, right inferior and superior parietal lobule, left insula, left caudate and left brain stem."[3] In other words, far from a simplistic explanation for the feeling of transcendence, the nuns' brain activity showed a complex pattern inconsistent with a simple explanation about what happens when we pray.

Obviously the experience of the Montreal nuns neither confirms nor denies the existence of God. Instead, their experience shows that what happens to us when we pray resists simplistic explanations because the brain is active far beyond mere emotion.

As a result of this research, we can prove conclusively that prayer has the power to alter significantly the activity of the brain and how we feel and think about the world around us. Beyond the internal, positive feelings and emotional sense of well-being that accompanies prayer, is it possible for prayer to change the circumstances around us?

For the answer to that, we have to leave the postmodern complexities of sprawling Montreal and travel to another busy city in the ancient world, located near a commercial lake. Here we find the densely populated, multicultural, and commercially prosperous town of Capernaum, where the newest resident was Jesus of Nazareth.

Jesus in Prayer
Mark 1:21–35

In the motionless darkness when waking from a dead sleep, the mind can be uncertain about whether it is early morning or only the middle of the night; but in the stillness of those moments, Jesus wrestled Himself from the bed and slipped out of the house to be absolutely alone. During several months of the year, the night air around Capernaum is chilled by the frequent winds that blow through the deep, natural basin that creates the freshwater lake fed by the Jordan River called the Sea of Galilee.

It would perhaps be a few hours before the merchants, families, and travelers would crowd the busy streets of Capernaum, but Jesus was up long before daylight, no doubt covered by His customary Jewish prayer shawl, so He could pray in secret. Jesus of Nazareth had always been a man of prayer.

The Sabbath had been anything but restful the day before, and no one would have criticized Jesus if He had chosen to sleep a few hours longer. But He planned to meet with God in prayer in those early morning hours, and He wanted no distractions or interruptions. Concerning that morning vigil Mark said, "And rising very early in the morning, while it was still dark, He departed and went out to a desolate place, and there He prayed" (Mark 1:35). The day before had started early for Jesus and His new followers as they made their way to the synagogue, the spiritual center of gravity for the Jewish people, where nearly everyone from the city attended the service.

The synagogue of Capernaum was distinctly different from the one Jesus had known as a boy growing up in Nazareth. Capernaum was one of Northern Israel's largest cities, and Nazareth was one of its smallest, so the two houses of worship reflected those differences. Only a few families attended the synagogue in Nazareth while the one in Capernaum was much larger to accommodate the wealthy business owners and many others who lived nearby.

Not only was Capernaum's synagogue large; it was beautiful. But that day something ugly had come to the worship service. While Jesus was teaching, a demon-possessed man disrupted the service with shrieks and out-bursts directed at Jesus. With no hesitation Jesus subdued the man victimized by an unclean spirit by demanding the spirit leave the man, which it did immediately. The people standing around the synagogue watching this odd scene unfold were amazed, and the people of Capernaum were almost universally determined to come to Jesus for help (Mark 1:23–28).

The synagogue was in the middle of a cluster of small homes, the archeological ruins of which are still obvious today. Tradition suggests that the home of Simon Peter was only a few yards from the synagogue, and there is no reason to doubt that. Peter and his brother, Andrew, were origi-nally from a nearby fishing village where they operated a prosperous fishing business in Bethsaida. Peter also owned a home in the more cosmopolitan city of Capernaum. Jesus spent the rest of the Sabbath in Simon Peter's house.

While Jesus was there that day, He healed Peter's mother-in-law and later a city full of demon-possessed and sick people who crowded at the door for deliverance and healing. It must have taken hours. It was a long day. But Jesus offered no excuses the next morning during those pitch-black hours before daylight when He kept His commitment to pray on what would have felt, for Him, like a Monday morning after a long day at church!

Almost twenty times the Gospels refer specifically to Jesus in prayer. Often He prayed through the night or when others had fallen asleep, as in Gethsemane. Before choosing His apostles, He prayed. He prayed with His disciples. He prayed before performing miracles. He prayed in public and He prayed in private. He even prayed while He was on the cross! The earliest followers of Jesus were Jewish men who had been trained and surrounded by prayer all of their lives, but when they saw the perpetual commitment of Jesus in prayer, they asked Him to teach them to pray! Are we any less in need of His instruction today?

Jesus Models the Priority of Prayer (v. 35)

Mark's description of the busyness of the previous day and the careful specificity of words regarding the time when Jesus left the house for prayer paints a portrait of His devotion. The exact wording of the Greek text describes a time between 3:00 a.m. and 6:00 a.m. Mark also insists that it was "exceedingly" early, still dark. Perhaps the idea is that it was closer to 3:00 a.m. than to 6:00 a.m. The Greek word for "dark" is *nux* from which we get our word *nocturnal*. It was pitch-black!

This early-morning prayer in the dark points to the priority Jesus of Nazareth placed on prayer. Think about it: Jesus felt He needed hours in prayer, and due to His busy schedule He had to create opportunities for time alone with God. His time in prayer was a strategic commitment. His devotion reminds us: If you're too busy to pray, you're too busy.

If Jesus placed such a high priority on prayer in His own life, what must He expect from those who follow Him? His entire life was intended as a model for us to emulate.

How long, therefore, should a believer spend in daily prayer? To offer a suggested time invariably invites us to follow the undesirable footsteps of the Pharisees, the same legalists Jesus was repeatedly forced to condemn! Yet a review of biblical material presents a compelling set of spiritual biographies that describe faithful men and women committed to endless hours of prayer.

Abraham built altars for prayer and spent so much time in communion with God that he almost single-handedly introduced the world to the radical concept of monotheism. Jacob wrestled in prayer throughout the night at Peniel. Moses on two occasions spent forty days praying on a desolate mountainside in the desert of the Sinai Peninsula. Hannah poured her soul into desperate prayer for months, or perhaps years, until God heard her and responded with the blessing of a child. Elijah fasted and prayed for forty days. Daniel prayed so regularly his enemies used it as a way to conspire against him. When Saul was rejected as king, Samuel prayed through the night. Ezra prayed and fasted for days and led the nation to do the same. Nehemiah prayed for weeks as he sought God's help.

If the narratives woven from the lives of Old Testament heroes of faith influence us at all, we cannot ignore the similarity they share at this point: they prayed for hours, days, weeks, and throughout their lives. Jesus was following a pattern of commitment to prayer that stretches back to the genesis of the Jewish people. At the same time He excelled as the ultimate model of prayer.

Reflecting on the priority of Jesus should spur each of us strategically to commit more time each day dedicated to prayer. What will you do differently, starting now, if you really believe Jesus prioritizes prayer?

Jesus Models Privacy in Prayer (v. 35)

The British evangelist Leonard Ravenhill once famously observed, "The secret of prayer is praying in secret."[4] The word in verse 35 describing the privacy Jesus was seeking for prayer—variously translated as "a desolate place," (ESV), "a solitary place" (NIV), and "a secluded place" (NASB)—is one Mark already used in chapter 1 to describe the setting for Jesus' most intense experience in prayer.

The Greek word *eremos* (v. 35) is the same one used in Mark to describe the desert region where Jesus spent forty days fasting and praying in the Judean Desert (vv.12–13). The area around Capernaum, however, is not a desert. It is fertile farmland and green hills around the Sea of Galilee. Clearly the word can mean "deserted" as well as "desert." Do we see here a subtle implication that Jesus wanted to recreate the spiritual intensity and solitude of those forty days again, if only for a few hours, in the midst of a busy schedule of ministry? Perhaps He did. At any rate Jesus exemplified on numerous occasions the importance of secret prayer, away from distractions and well-intended people who might come between Him and God. If Jesus could retreat from the life-and-death importance of His work, we certainly must learn to do the same. Time alone with God must supersede all other commitments and relationships if we intend to develop a prayer life like His.

Jesus Models the Purpose of Prayer (vv. 36–39)

The silence of Jesus in prayer was shattered when the always gregarious and usually brash Simon Peter crashed into the serene setting in an apparent rush, oblivious to the fact that the Son of God was worshipping the Father. I can almost hear the frantic follower, concerned only with his agenda, challenging Jesus for what must have seemed to him as an oversight—that Jesus would be alone when so many people demanded an audience with Him (vv. 36–37)!

The book of Mark, the shortest of the Gospels, seems to be written with a breathless insistence on what happens next, so the author rarely examines the teaching portions of Jesus' ministry. He does not reveal what Jesus was praying about, yet it may be obvious in our Lord's response to Peter. When challenged by Peter to come back from His prayer retreat and offer additional ministry in Capernaum, Jesus cast an alternative vision for His future. "And he said to them, 'Let us go on to the next towns that I may preach there also, for that is why I came out'" (Mark 1:38). The purpose of His prayers may have been about reaching more people with His message. At least that was the first thing on His mind when He was interrupted from prayer! Frankly, it is almost impossible to imagine Jesus praying about anything else given the fact that it was He who said, "The Son of Man came to seek and to save the lost" (Luke 19:10).

Conclusion

Whether it is a neuroscientist mapping how brain activity is altered during prayer or the story of the Savior rising from prayer to change the world, it is clear that prayer changes us. Prayer not only changes something inside us, but it also leads us to change the world around us. It is true: "Prayer moves the hand that moves the world."

For Memory and Meditation

"And rising very early in the morning, while it was still dark, he departed and went out to a desolate place, and there he prayed." Mark 1:35

———

[1] Mario Beauregard and Denyse O'Leary, *The Spiritual Brain* (New York: HarperOne, 2007), xiii, xvi.

[2] Ibid., 263.

[3] Ibid., 275.

[4] Leonard Ravenhill, *Why Revival Tarries* (Bloomington, MN: Bethany House, 1987), 26.

Followers

Focal Text: Matthew 4:18–22

An artist can see a finished masterpiece before a single brushstroke leaves a drop of paint on a blank canvas. Likewise, a sculptor working with stone sees the figure the stone will become before the hammer ever touches the chisel. Even though man has sculpted and created art for all of his existence, with today's power of computer animation, it is easier than ever to see a work of art finished before it even begins. The mathematical term *hyperseeing*[1] describes the ability to view a three-dimensional object from a single vantage point. Computer simulations make that easier to do, but sculptors have been doing it in their imaginations for centuries. For instance, when the sculptor Gutzon Borglum conceived of and created the presidential faces on Mount Rushmore, he tried to describe how it was possible for an artist to visualize something so mammoth. Speaking with overstated bravado, the artist said, "I must think, see, feel, and draw in Thor's dimension." In other words the artist saw himself and his ability to conceive of the unseen as if he were a god.

The only person who had ever carved a mountain into art at the time was Borglum himself. It required using dynamite to remove the half-million tons of granite, using carving techniques previously unheard of and taking fourteen years to complete. It is almost impossible to imagine how Borglum conceived of the project. For instance, the face of Washington alone is sixty feet long, his nose is twenty feet long, and his eyes are eleven feet across. Nothing like it had ever been done before. Gutzon Borglum never heard of the term *hyperseeing*, yet he epitomized it when he looked at a mountainside in the Black Hills of South Dakota and envisioned and eventually sculpted four lifelike presidential busts, the largest sculpture in the world.

Artists, however, aren't the only people capable of hyperseeing. Jesus of Nazareth may have never sculpted a work of art, although as a carpenter He was, no doubt, a craftsman. Yet He did have the eye of an artist. He could see a finished project before it ever began, especially as it relates to the lives of those who follow Him.

The Future Jesus Saw
Matthew 4:18–22

Walking beside the usually quiet, rippling waters along the coastline of the Sea of Galilee, Jesus could see men doing what had been done for centuries. Early in the morning before dawn, they began the process of casting weighted nets over the sides of their twenty-five-foot cedar and oak boats in the hopes of catching a school of sardines or the larger, bony musht fish, common in the lake. But Jesus saw more than hardworking fishermen; He saw the future. He could hypersee what did not appear obvious to anyone else at the time. Jesus saw a worldwide outreach that would continue until the end of human history ignited by His followers, even though that morning by the water, He didn't yet have any followers!

Four men were busy with their nets that morning and were the focus of Jesus' attention. Jesus was familiar with them, but they were not yet His full-time followers. They were still preoccupied with their prosperous partnership, fishing the Sea of Galilee. All of their lives were about to change, however, as Jesus had plans for them.

The Men Who Followed Jesus
John 1:35-42

Andrew and John were more than business partners; they were seekers. Their desire to know God's plans for them had led them to align with the enigmatic prophet, John the Baptist. In fact, their first contact with Jesus occurred while they were traveling and studying with the confrontational prophet, far to the south of their lakeside business and homes. "Bethany Across the Jordan" is probably located in a narrow, shallow part of the Jordan River, perhaps as far south as Jericho. Even if it is in a location north of that spot, as some speculate, it was a considerable distance from a fishing business and implies the seriousness of the disciples who were willing to follow John the Baptist.

One day as Jesus was walking near where John was baptizing, Andrew and John, the brother of James, were standing with John the Baptist when he saw Jesus and declared Him to be the sacrificial Lamb who would eventually bear the sins of the world. The two disciples of the Baptist were intrigued and struck up a conversation with Jesus. They were obviously humbled at the thought that this man might be the Messiah, and their first words reflected that sincere and innocent modesty in Jesus' presence. When Jesus noticed the two men tagging along, He turned and asked them a question dripping with intuition and meaning beyond the immediate context: "What are you seeking?" (John 1:38). For those drawn to the spiritual issues of existence, perhaps no question is more profound or baffling. What are we seeking? What do we perceive to be missing from our lives? What is that almost universal sense that "there must be something more"?

Andrew and John were both influential and successful men with a business that required them to employ laborers and support two generations of families (the business was also partially owned by their brothers and Andrew's father). In other words, they had financial security along with a support system of family members and friends. Their lives were far from ordinary, impoverished, or solitary. They were gregarious men who easily and naturally attracted others. We would say they were "born leaders." Yet they sensed something missing from their lives. Jesus knew that. He knew they were interested in something far deeper than an afternoon discussing theology or the politics of the day. They were ready to follow someone who could lead them to God.

Jesus' invitation that day to those two allows us a glimpse into His personality. When the two followers asked Him where He was staying, Jesus was warm and accommodating. He advised them simply, "Come and see." The rest of the day was spent getting to know Him and listening to His profound and refreshingly original ideology. Whatever was discussed that day was convincing. Andrew was determined to persuade his brother that Jesus was the fulfillment of Hebrew prophecy. He told Simon Peter, "We have found the Messiah" (1:41).

Andrew's excitement about the identity of Jesus gives us the clue about what he had been missing in his otherwise full life. He and John, the brother of James, had previously become followers of John the Baptist for the same reason. The Baptist had emerged in Israel as an unexpected force of charisma and spiritual fierceness no one had seen in generations. He had probably studied at the monastic enclave of zealous pilgrims attached to a community near the Dead Sea, today known as Qumran. While the Baptist differed with some of the unusual tenets of the mysterious group, he nonetheless reflected accurately their insistence on obedience to the will of God, their love for Scripture, their practice of full immersion in water as a sign of ritual purification, and an austere lifestyle that preferred the desert and viewed the cities—and the established religious leadership within them—with suspicion. For John the Baptist and those who followed him, the Messianic Age had arrived and, perhaps along with it, a time of God's judgment and the immediate necessity of repentance.

The spiritual clarity reflected in John the Baptist rang true for Andrew and his business partner, John. It was irresistible. What they sensed in John the Baptist would be eclipsed, however, by the powerful attraction they, and so many others, would eventually find in the personality, sterling character, and lively teaching of Jesus.

The Decision to Follow
Luke 5:1–11

Jesus was a preacher and a teacher, and His message was appealing to a growing number of people because He taught "the word of God" (v. 1). As He walked and taught beside the Sea of Galilee, the throng of people who were gathering to hear Jesus kept pressing closer in on one another and on Him. He decided some distance between Himself and the crowd could bring order and perhaps safety to the mass of people and assure that everyone had a chance to hear Him.

The men He had met beside the baptismal site near Jericho, and their brothers, were now back in Galilee and busy cleaning their nets by the shore when Jesus stepped into one of their boats. He asked Simon, Andrew's brother, to help Him by pushing back from the shore. By requesting assistance from Simon, Jesus was engaging a man into service who would later become the leader among Jesus' other followers and one of the two most important figures in the early church. Of course Simon Peter had no way of knowing that at the time. Just as Jesus often calls us to help Him where we have the natural gifting to do so, even so His plans for us always involve more than our natural talents. He uses us where He finds us; and, as in Peter's example, what Jesus does with us beyond those early assignments are opportunities to serve, which are almost always unpredictable and far beyond our natural expectations.

After teaching the people, Jesus turned His full attention to Peter and the others who had entered the boat with Him. He urged them to go out deeper. The Sea of Galilee is thirteen miles long, up to eight miles wide, and reaches depths of nearly 150 feet. It is full of fish. Jesus pointed them to a school of fish that rivaled any they had seen in their lifetimes. Peter called for the other boat to join them, and together they greedily netted so much the boats started to sink! Only then did they realize they were part of a miracle involving the overwhelming generosity of Jesus.

Peter was conscience stricken and ashamed, but Jesus used the moment to drive home a point. Even if you get everything you've ever wanted in life, if Jesus is calling you in another direction, the abundance this world offers in place of God's best will inevitably leave you empty. At that point Jesus offered Peter and the others a new life. In that teachable moment, when the boats were overloaded with squirming fish, Jesus promised to make Peter a catcher of men's souls. No wonder Peter and Andrew, and later James and John, immediately left the security of the family fishing business and started across the countryside following Jesus. Whatever benefits there were in staying by the boats were quickly forgotten. Jesus was calling and they had to go!

After two thousand years we read the story of the first disciples through the lens of church and spiritual history, which can sometimes be sentimental or even spiritualized through our retelling of the event. But those men actually lived. They had families, jobs, responsibilities, and plans of their own for their futures. What then was so compelling about Jesus that businessmen with families dropped everything and left?

Certainly the miracle of the historic catch of fish is a factor. Jesus had power the early followers had never seen before. Who wouldn't be intrigued by the possibilities inherent in following a miracle worker? Fishing was their work. It could be laborious, unproductive, and disappointing at times. In fact, the miracle itself followed a night of fishing that produced no results (Luke 5:5). Jesus appeared and made it all so easy, but is that why they followed Him? The text offers us no reason to assume that. Without discounting the persuasive power of the miraculous, there is another, more obvious reason to abandon everything to follow Jesus.

All four Gospels mention the calling of the disciples, but only Luke records the miraculous catch of fish. Three of the gospels, however, mention another aspect of the calling that seems to explain the reason the men followed Jesus. He gave them a mission.

"For he and all who were with him were astonished at the catch of fish that they had taken, and so also were James and John, sons of Zebedee, who were partners with Simon. And Jesus said to Simon, 'Do not be afraid; from now on you will be catching men.' And when they had brought their boats to land, they left everything and followed him" (Luke 5:9–11). It was the vision of influencing others—"catching men"—that motivated the early followers to become Jesus' first disciples. The miraculous catch was merely an illustration of what they could expect. They must have remembered that day, three years later, when thousands of people turned to Christ when they preached at Pentecost (Acts 2:38–42).

Today the reasons for following Jesus haven't changed. He still offers His followers the opportunity to make a difference in others' lives. What would you be willing to change today if you knew Jesus wanted to use you to influence the people around you for His glory? You can still discover a purpose in your future, closer to the heart of Jesus than any other on earth, if you follow Him and "fish" for people!

For Memory and Meditation

"And he said to them, 'Follow me, and I will make you fishers of men.'" Matthew 4:19

---

[1] Thanks to David H. Roper for the idea for this illustration: David H. Roper, "Hyperseeing," *Our Daily Bread*, February 12 2014, www. odb.org

Miracles

Focal Text: Matthew 14:13–21

Long before recent restorations turned Times Square into a trendy, family-friendly tourist destination, the streets were dark, dirty, and dangerous. The decadence of sex clubs, pornographic theaters, poverty, and addiction was everywhere. Children on the streets, still in their early teens, were selling sex for drug money. If junkies wandering the night wanted to buy heroin, somebody lurking in the shadows of a nearby alley would be there to sell the drug, along with whatever else the buyer might crave. The famous theater district of New York City had become the rotten core of the Big Apple. Law enforcement was overwhelmed by the size of the problem, and city government's efforts to initiate lasting change had repeatedly failed. Times Square and 42nd Street didn't just need more laws. The area was almost too far gone. Nothing attempted so far had been able to turn the tide of systemic corruption. The city needed some kind of miracle.

David Wilkerson had come to New York City thirty years earlier to evangelize and minister to the violent gangs that filled the streets. After spending five years there, he wrote a book about his experiences, and *The Cross and the Switchblade* unexpectedly sold sixteen million copies. Wilkerson, a third-generation small-church pastor and a country preacher from rural Pennsylvania, was suddenly a celebrity. He started preaching across the United States to venues reaching thousands of people. He had relocated out of New York to a sprawling ranch in East Texas where he headquartered his growing preaching and addiction recovery ministry, which by then was known all over the world.

In 1986, as part of an evangelistic mission, he was back in Manhattan evangelizing in the streets near Times Square and 42nd Street. He was stunned by what he saw. New York was worse, it seemed to him, than when he had arrived in 1958. Something needed to be done. He started praying for a miracle. In 1986, at the age of fifty-five, David Wilkerson started Times Square Church; and before he died in 2011, the church had grown in attendance to more than eight thousand people every week. To grow a church from zero to eight thousand people in twenty years, led by a church planter in his mid-fifties, is nearly unheard of.

One late autumn night, long after the church building had been closed and locked for the evening, I was standing at the entrance of Times Square Church reading a well-lit marquee describing the history of what seems to be a miraculous example of church growth. Somehow I was oblivious to the stack of cardboard leaning against the church building near my feet until it started to move!

At night in New York City, businesses, apartments, cafés, and churches put their garbage on the sidewalks, and the trucks come all night through the city collecting it. That night was no exception. Perhaps that's why, with the sidewalks full of boxes and garbage bags, I paid no particular attention to the pile of cardboard Gerald was sleeping under on the drenched sidewalk beside the church.

Gerald was friendly, articulate, and oddly apologetic for being in the shape he was in. As I handed him a few bucks and prayed for him, he told me the abbreviated version of his personal story of downward mobility. This wasn't the life he had hoped for, but there he was: sleeping on a sidewalk under a piece of cardboard waiting for morning. He knew someone from the church would help him. The church that had been started twenty-five years earlier to help people like Gerald was still known as a place where the helpless could find assistance. I said good-bye and walked away, Gerald thanking me as I left. It was a staggering moment of familiar frustration. If only there was a way more could be done for people like Gerald. He's just one of many in that city, across the country, and around the world who need something no handout can cure. He, and so many others, needs some kind of miracle.

The Miracle Worker

What do you suppose most people know about Jesus of Nazareth? Certainly most would associate Jesus with His death on the cross, and many remember that He was a teacher. In addition, most people know that Jesus performed miracles. He raised the dead, cast out demons, walked on water, and healed the sick—all miraculously. Of all of His miracles (fewer than forty are specifically mentioned in Scripture), what do you think was His most important miracle? For me, at first glance, raising Lazarus from the dead, healthy and whole, after the dead man had been decomposing in the tomb for three days stands out as most impressive, but only one Gospel even mentions it. He calmed storms by talking to them. He turned drinking water into wine, gave blind men sight for the first time in their lives, and sent demons out of men and into pigs. Any of these could qualify as the most important of His miracles, but only one miracle is recorded in all four Gospels.

Feeding five thousand men with only a few small fish and two pieces of bread is the miracle the Gospel writers saw as the supernatural high-water mark in the ministry of Jesus. Why?

Feeding Five Thousand

When Jesus performed the miracle of feeding the five thousand, He had a broken heart. John the Baptist, His cousin and the forerunner who had baptized Him and announced Him to Israel, had been brutally murdered in a state-sanctioned execution. After learning that John's head had been severed and handed on a plate to a young woman in Herod's ruthless and psychologically damaged family, Jesus retreated from public to pray in private and consider the future (Matt. 14:1–13).

Jesus loved solitude. The number of times the Gospels refer to Jesus alone are too numerous to be ignored or dismissed as coincidence (Matt. 4:1–11; Mark 1:35; Luke 6:12; John 6:15). He spent the time in prayer and often needed the opportunity to refocus others' expectations about His ministry. In addition to the solo pilgrimages into private places, He also took brief excursions with a few of His closest and most trusted disciples (Matt. 26:36–46; Mark 9:2–13; Luke 9:18–20). These side trips always included prayer and usually were for the purpose of getting His group away from the influences of the crowds swelling around the ministry of Jesus and the misunderstandings that naturally surrounded Him. When He retreated after the news of John's bloody death, it seems clear Jesus needed time to process what had happened, reflect on the implications for His ministry going forward, and rest (Mark 6:31). The events described by Matthew regarding Jesus' response to the news about

John are vivid in the literal Greek text. "And hearing, Jesus withdrew from that place in a ship into a deserted place" (Matt. 14:13, author's translation). Jesus was getting away as a direct result of John's death.

Retreats for Jesus were routinely interrupted by the pressing demands of a growing ministry. His desire to be alone after the news about John was an example of the near impossibility of Jesus' being away from the crowds for long. He knew of a lonely place near Bethsaida, on the far northern tip of the Sea of Galilee (Luke 9:10). It was the hometown of several of the disciples and the location of the fishing business of Peter, Andrew, James, and John. It was just east of the Jordan River and located near a remote area, thick with grass, near the town. There Jesus hoped to spend time in prayer, but the curious crowds anticipated His whereabouts and followed Him by foot to the region. As soon as Jesus saw them, His own heart, still tender from the news of John's death, was moved with compassion for the people eagerly following Him. His compassion—a New Testament word describing a physical, internal response brought about by powerful emotion—seems therefore to be the basis of His most frequently recorded miracle.

After a day of hearing Jesus' teaching and witnessing healings, the huge crowd gathered spontaneously and lingered as the sun started to set. The disciples sensed a developing dilemma. Several of them were from the fishing village of Bethsaida near the large remote area where the day's events had occurred. They knew the town was much too small to provide food for the thousands of people present. Matthew tells us there were five thousand men not counting the women and children also present (14:21). Obviously the crowd could have numbered several thousand more than the five thousand men. The ministry of Jesus was taking on a family festival atmosphere. Providing up to ten thousand impromptu meals seems virtually impossible even today. The coordination and distribution alone, the lines, the amount of food needed, and the preparation time necessary would require significant advanced planning, not to mention the need to secure the food. None of that had occurred. The situation was out of human control. But Jesus was about to display the power of the miraculous in a way none of His biographers could forget.

One of the characteristics of Jesus in the New Testament was His insistence that His followers take responsibility for ministry. The disciples, who were obviously anxious about what might happen with so many people lacking food and shelter, advised Jesus to send the crowd away. Jesus, however, aware that those same men would lead the early church and needed greater faith, challenged them to feed the crowd themselves. How bizarre must that request have seemed to the worried men? There were a dozen of them and perhaps ten thousand or more hungry people. They were outnumbered a thousand to one! What was Jesus thinking? Was He taunting them? Or, knowing what He knew, was Jesus preparing His disciples to believe for things that seem impossible and humanly speaking out of reach? Does Jesus still look at what we call "impossible" and confidently assure us we can do it? Do miracles start where every human resource is insipid?

By this time the disciples knew Jesus was unlike anyone else they had known, and so they tried to stay engaged with His reasoning even though they were obviously clueless about what He had planned. The Gospels offer humorous glimpses into the disciples' clumsy efforts to obey the impossible insistence of Jesus that they provide the food. One of them examined the group bank account and came up with two hundred denarii and speculated it would hardly be enough to buy a fraction of the people a bite each (John 6:7). Another found a boy who had a lunch: two sardines from the Sea of Galilee and five hard, thick, flat barley cakes (loaves of bread) were available, and the boy was willing to share (John 6:8). The fish and barley loaves were a common meal for the Galileans. How small the disciples must have felt holding a child's lunch and looking back at a hungry crowd of more than ten thousand people. At the point at which it was obvious human resources were insufficient, Jesus began the greatest miracle of His ministry.

The Simplicity of the Impossible

The miracle itself is described in the New Testament with an economy of words. One verse in Matthew says Jesus instructed the crowd to be seated. He then blessed the food, broke the bread into fragments, and the disciples distributed it to the crowds. That's it. The supernatural doesn't become sensational. Jesus took two sardines and five biscuits and fed five thousand men along with their wives and children. When everyone had eaten all they wanted, there was more left over than when they started.

What do we know about Jesus as a result of the miracle? Why did the four Gospels record this miracle when no other miracle and almost no other event is recorded in all four?

Most Bible students see a comparison between Jesus' feeding the multitude and Moses' providing manna in the desert (Exod. 16:1–36). Both stories emphasize feeding a community miraculously. One difference, however, is that while the Jews in the wilderness were completely dependent on the manna for survival, Jesus' miracle wasn't really a matter of life and death. The people were, after all, from nearby villages and within walking distance of home. No one wants children to go hungry, but the hunger was inconvenient rather than life threatening. This miracle of Jesus therefore highlights His warm, personal compassion. He delighted in helping.

In addition, the miracle shows that Jesus easily does what is absolutely impossible. This miracle reveals the authority of Jesus over the laws that govern normal life. Whereas we have limited, nonreplenishing resources, Jesus effortlessly feeds thousands of people with only a single child's lunch portion. The fact that He can do the impossible draws us to wonder: Who is He? The miracles were signs pointing to something other than themselves. They alert us to the fact that God is in our midst.

Finally, Jesus' challenge remains: "You give them something to eat" (Matt. 14:16). In every generation we see hopeless situations waiting for the church to do the impossible. Like David Wilkerson praying God would send someone to do something in the theater district, only to sense God's call to do it himself, the challenges in front of us may be merely our unclaimed miracles waiting for us to respond. We can bring the impossible to Jesus, and He can do it with ease. In His presence miracles still happen.

For Memory and Meditation
"And they all ate and were satisfied. And they took up twelve baskets full of the broken pieces left over." Matthew 14:20

I AM

Focal Text: John 8:48–59

He looked over his shoulder out of habit after all the years of being on the run. As a fugitive, he was always wary of strangers, and as a result he stayed to himself as much as possible. As far as the law knew, he was nonexistent. He was "off the grid," and he liked it that way. He was wanted by the authorities back home, and he was never sure how far or how long they were willing to look for him in order to arrest him and take him back.

Maybe so much time had passed he was a cold case by now. In any event he could never be too careful. In the heat of the moment, he had killed a man in a brawl that should have never involved him. As soon as the word got out that he was the perpetrator, he panicked and ran. For years he hid in the most remote place he could find south of the border, working in a menial job no one who had known him before could have ever imagined he would do during all of those years since he had disappeared. It was a near-perfect getaway. He never planned to go back home. Then something happened that changed everything.

Moses had plenty of time to think about what he had done. He had time to reflect and time to regret. In his reclusive hiding place he had led a lonely life as a shepherd for forty years in Midian, a moonscape of a desert in modern northwest Arabia, near the Gulf of Aqaba. How many times his mind must have wandered back to the days of power and privilege in the court of Pharaoh. Moses was raised as an adopted grandson of the most powerful leader on earth, and his early life was one of luxury and authority. Following sheep around the desert was never his ambition. It was a good refuge though, as he hid in plain sight following that terrible day in Egypt when he intervened in a skirmish between a Hebrew slave and an Egyptian.

Days for him now were anything but luxurious. They were uneventful and monotonous as months melted into decades. Then one day he saw something new. That in itself was a welcome change! In the distance he saw smoke from a small fire, but this fire was unusual because it blazed without interruption. He saw no apparent reason for the fire, and it never burned down. Curiously the fire did not consume the bush it had ignited.

History changed that day because God spoke to Moses from the flames of the burning bush and called him to go back to Egypt, rescue the people of Israel, and lead them back to God's promised land (Exod. 3:1–17). Moses balked and insisted he couldn't do it. For one thing, he couldn't even say who had sent him on the mission. At that point God revealed to Moses His covenant name, by which He would be known to the Jews forever. He would henceforth be known to them as "Yahweh," the Hebrew word for "I AM" (Exod. 3:13–14).

Over the centuries, leading up to Jesus' time, that name, "I AM," became so revered, the Jews refused even to pronounce it for fear they would blaspheme the name of God. By revealing Himself as "I AM," God made clear that He is self-existent. Who but God could honestly make a statement like that?

Jesus—the I AM
John 8:48–59

Jesus of Nazareth had a way of infuriating the religious leaders of His day. He was constantly saying and doing nontraditional things in a culture that thrived on tradition. On more than one occasion His readiness to confront their treasured opinions led them to a furious willingness to kill Him on the spot. The day He claimed to be God was one of those days!

If Jesus had claimed to be a prophet or a representative of God, He would have been, in that sense, like other godly men over the centuries. But Jesus of Nazareth went much further than claiming to be a spokesman or prophet of God. As a result, the religious leaders wanted Him dead. When He claimed to be "I AM," He crossed a line no one had ever risked crossing. At that point the Jews felt an obligation to stop debating Him and stone Him instead.

The entire eighth chapter of John shows Jesus in a contentious, ongoing debate where strong words and accusations were expressed by both sides. Christians often overlook the fact that Jesus was robust in His disputes; and even before claiming to be God that day, He had accused His critics of being sons of the devil (John 8:44). In response they hurled racial slurs and accused Jesus of being demon possessed (v. 48). The mood of the argument was getting ugly, but Jesus had much more to say, and the debate would end with an attempted murder!

The "I AM"
John 6–15

Jesus had used the words "I am" in conjunction with picturesque descriptions of Himself in seven unique settings. He said: "I am the bread of life" (6:35); "I am the light of the world" (8:12); "I am the door" (10:9); "I am the good shepherd" (10:11); "I am the resurrection and the life" (11:25); "I am the way, and the truth, and the life" (14:6); and "I am the true vine" (15:1). These descriptions are powerful self-portraits of a man certain of who He is and what He came to do. A careful review of each of the statements demonstrates that Jesus sees Himself as one of a kind: *the* bread, *the* light, *the* resurrection and *the* life, *the* way, *the* truth, *the* life. What kind of man describes Himself as "*the* life"? Who sees Himself as *the* resurrection? Can there be any doubt about what Jesus meant when He declared Himself to be *the* way?

As direct as those pronouncements are, in the minds of Jesus' opponents, they were not as inflammatory as His simple statement, "I AM." After two thousand years the significance of that statement might be somewhat lost on a Western audience, but it was not lost on the Pharisees in the temple that day. They knew exactly what God had revealed to Moses hundreds of years earlier. By repeating those words and insisting they referred to Him, Jesus was now claiming to be the God who appeared to Moses in the burning bush. Jesus claimed to be the God of Israel, and that was the line the religious leaders would not allow any person to cross. It was, after all, an astounding claim.

What Abraham Saw
John 8:52–57

Abraham was the father of Judaism. He lived approximately eighteen hundred to two thousand years before Jesus. Without equivocation Jesus claimed Abraham "rejoiced" to see Jesus' "day." To the religious leaders that statement was laughable. They pointedly reminded the young man from Nazareth He was not even fifty years old! How could Abraham see Jesus? That is a good question. What did Jesus mean?

There are at least three possibilities, and perhaps we should accept all of them as the viable answer to the question. When God called Abraham, He promised Him a day would come when "all the families of the earth shall be blessed" (Gen. 12:3). In that sense Abraham "saw" or anticipated a day in the future when his obedience would lead to a worldwide blessing. Ultimately that blessing of the Gentiles would come through the Jewish Messiah.

Next there was a day when the "angel of the Lord," appearing as a man, came to visit Abraham. The scene is powerful because God spoke face-to-face with the patriarch. They walked, they talked, and they discussed the mercy and judgment of God (Gen. 18:1–33). Two Hebrew verbs describe the intimacy of the scene. The story unfolds with angelic visitors walking away to leave, but the Lord stayed with Abraham. The text says, "But Abraham still stood before the Lord" (Gen. 18:22). The word "stood" can mean he physically remained standing there. It does mean that. But it can also include the idea of remaining in the presence of God or "persisting" in God's presence. The phrase says he stood "before" the Lord. The Hebrew word translated "before" is actually the word *face*, which is often interpreted to mean God's presence. In other words, Abraham persisted in the face—the very presence—of God!

The second word is equally powerful as a description of spiritual fellowship with the Lord. "Then Abraham drew near" (Gen. 18:23). That word describes an intimate scene when Abraham got as close to the physical presence of God as any human being had been since Adam walked with God in the garden of Eden! Was it Jesus in a preincarnation appearance that Abraham saw that day when God became a man?

Finally, in Genesis 22, in the provocative drama when Abraham offered Isaac on the altar, the boy asked his father about the absence of the sacrifice. Abraham, with a broken heart but with his faith fixed on the resurrection (Heb. 11:18–19), promised his son that "God will provide for himself the lamb" (Gen. 22:1–8). Those words, when we think of the cross that would come centuries later, are both poignant and prophetic! In these ways Abraham, as a prophet and as the spiritual head of the Jewish religion, "saw" the "day" of Jesus the Messiah.

Before Abraham Was
John 8:58–59

The Pharisees cynically mocked Jesus for saying Abraham had seen His day, but the mirth and sarcasm stopped abruptly when Jesus responded. He said, "Before Abraham was, I am." That statement to a Jewish audience steeped in Old Testament teaching could be interpreted only one way: Jesus of Nazareth claimed to be God. Perhaps nowhere in the New Testament is He clearer about it. Of course, the claim of divinity supports one of the main emphases of John's Gospel, namely the deity of Christ. In fact, while the other Gospels write with a kind of "Messianic secret" view of Jesus' identity, John opened his Gospel with the revelation that Jesus was the eternal Word of God, who is, in fact, God! (John 1:1–2)

The claim of Jesus that He was, and is, the God of the Old Testament, temporarily recognized by human form, makes Him different from any of the other Hebrew prophets. They represented God. They knew God. They served God. Jesus is God.

As a result of His self-revelation, our response to Jesus has to be different from our response to any other person who ever lived. We come to Him by faith believing what He said, or we must eventually dismiss Him. There can be no intellectual integrity in a middle ground of merely tolerating Him if He isn't who He claimed to be. If He had claimed to be a prophet or only an ambassador of God, we could evaluate Him from that vantage point. But claiming to be God is another story. He either is or He isn't.

If He is God, no serious seeker of truth can choose to ignore Him. The person who honestly wants to know God is left with no alternative but to follow Jesus. If, on the other hand, He isn't God, then He was either deceived Himself, or He deliberately misrepresented Himself. In either case we would have no reason to follow Him. After all, if He claimed to be God and wasn't, and if knew He wasn't, then He lied. Why would any decent person, if he is interested in finding the truth, knowingly commit himself to following a liar?

If He claimed to be God and wasn't but didn't know He wasn't, He was deranged. Have you ever known anyone who actually thought he was the one true God? That would be a delusional psychiatric patient in need of medical care. That isn't a person we turn to for spiritual guidance. It certainly isn't a person we point our children, family, and friends to for spiritual help.

So with spiritual truth at stake and our own souls in the balance, if Jesus was either lying or psychotic, my advice is to run from Him. He would have nothing to offer you. If He isn't who He claimed to be, then His delusion or His distortion of the truth, whichever it was, has ruined the lives of billions of people who have trusted Him for forgiveness and eternal life, which He promised. But obviously, if He isn't who He claimed to be, He cannot deliver on those promises. He isn't even a good person if He isn't who He claimed to be. In fact, He would actually be a leading candidate for one of the worst people who ever lived. If He misrepresented Himself, He has led billions of people astray.

But, if He is who He claimed to be, you should serve Him, follow Him, and love Him. That becomes the ultimate question directly confronting every person who honestly considers His claims, namely, who is Jesus? That's the question His claims force us to answer. Is He a fraud, a psychotic, or the Lord of all?

The attempt to stone Jesus that day in the temple failed, but His enemies would get another chance. Today, two thousand years later, we know that every effort to stop His message has utterly failed. More people follow Jesus of Nazareth today than at any time in history, and people are beginning to follow Him around the world at a faster pace than at any time since the first century.

When God first revealed Himself as the "I AM," it was to a lonely old shepherd on the back side of a desert in the sunbaked sands of Arabia. Now, all over the world we know His name is Jesus, and He always was, still is, and always will be the great "I AM"!

For Memory and Meditation

"Jesus said to them, 'Truly, truly, I say to you, before Abraham was, I am.'" John 8:58

Disciples of the Fourth Cross

Focal Text: Luke 9:21–26

Even the children were exposed to the sight of the men writhing in agony. Wives were forced to stand helplessly by while their husbands were dragged away, sometimes crying and begging for their lives; and yet there was nothing the broken women could do. Strong men, usually fearless, were left with no options but silently to curse the government or offer a prayer for the condemned. When the Romans condemned a man to die on the cross, it was deliberately public and intentionally ruthless. Nailing a human being to a cross and leaving him there for days to die in full view of his family and friends stands as one of the most bloodthirsty actions ever enforced by a government against its citizens. The cross was a death penalty; but it was slow, agonizing, humiliating, and torturous not only to the guilty prisoner but also to the psyche of the community where the cross was erected and used. Rome wanted it that way.

Most people know Jesus died on a cross, but He wasn't the only one. Four crosses are mentioned in the New Testament: the cross of the thief on the right of Jesus, the cross of the thief on His left, Jesus' cross, and your cross. No disciple is exempt. If you follow Jesus, you have to carry a cross. Therefore, you are called to be a disciple of the fourth cross.

Following Jesus is dangerous. People are killed for their faith. Many believers go to prison for years, and some never get out. Millions of Christians hide their faith from their families or their neighbors because it is against the law to believe what Jesus taught. It was bad in the first century, but it's even worse today.

In two-thirds of the nations of the world, followers of Jesus are culturally and legally harassed for their faith. Christians today are the most persecuted religious group on earth with 75 percent of the actions of brutality and religious intolerance worldwide aimed at them. In fact, more people were martyred for their Christian faith in the twentieth century than in the previous nineteen millennia combined.[1] The twenty-first century is starting out equally bad. Being a follower of Jesus is not safe. Yet the Christian movement is growing faster today, worldwide, than at any time in history, even though the cost of following Jesus has never been higher.

The High Cost of Following
Luke 9:18–26

In a private prayer retreat with His close-knit band of original followers, in the cool, high altitudes of northern Israel, Jesus asked one of the most poignant and personal questions of His entire ministry. He looked at His friends and inquired, "But who do you say I am?" (Luke 9:20). It was a breakthrough moment for the disciples when Peter, speaking on behalf of the group, blurted out, "The Christ of God" (Luke 9:20).

What followed was a strange mix of assurance and warning. Jesus agreed with Peter and assured him of blessing for his statement of faith (Matt. 16:17–19), but His mood suddenly shifted to a seriousness that foreshadowed His stern predictions for the future of His movement. His first prediction concerned His own violent death at the hands of His enemies in Jerusalem, along with the promise of His resurrection (Luke 9:22). His attention then switched to the lives of His followers. What He said next, while more obvious to us, must have shaken the prayer group to their core. He promised them each a cross (v. 23).

Crucifixion was a terrible way to die. It was brutal and inhumane and was the twisted brainchild of barbarian tribes on the fringes of civilization. Unfortunately, the Roman Empire had adopted the cross as a way of enforcing its will upon the large part of the world controlled by the caesars.[2]

The cross for Jesus wasn't jewelry or a topper for a steeple on a neighborhood church. It wasn't a tattoo on a rock star or an athlete. The cross for Jesus and His disciples meant only one thing: death. So, why did He tell His disciples they had to take up their cross in order to follow Him?

In one sense it should be more obvious to us today than it was to them then. Christian history is the story of martyrdom and persecution. The disciples couldn't know what we know, but they discovered it by experience. They all suffered and died for their faith, testimony, and devotion. Jesus prepared them for it. He alerted them to the cross ahead. Bearing a cross means the Christian life is a one-way journey. The promises of the Christian life for hope, salvation, faith, the gifts, and the joy—everything—comes from our willingness to carry a cross. While some bemoan their difficult or tragic circumstances as "the cross I have to bear," that view sounds as if bearing the cross is an impediment that slows us down in the Christian life. Or perhaps the "cross we have to bear" is a punishment of some kind. Nonsense! Bearing a cross is not an impediment to the Christian life;

bearing the cross *is* the Christian life. After reflecting on that truth years later, the apostle Paul would say, "I have been crucified with Christ. It is no longer I who live, but Christ who lives in me. And the life I now live in the flesh I live by faith in the Son of God, who loved me and gave himself for me" (Gal. 2:20).

Obviously there are no exceptions. "Cross takers" are not a special group of Christians. They are not an elite corps or "special ops" Christians. No. Jesus said, "If anyone would come after me...." There are no exceptions. The phrase "come after me" means all of those who choose to be followers of Jesus. The cross is for every believer. Taking up the cross is a brilliant and unsettling metaphor for the Christian life itself.

What then does it mean to take a cross for Christ? To more completely understand it today, we have to ask: What did it mean to the first disciples when they were alone that day with Jesus at Caesarea Philippi?

As previously observed, the cross was an instrument of death. If a man was condemned to die on the cross, it was the end of his personal freedom because it meant the end of his life. Carrying a cross to the place of crucifixion meant the condemned man had no other future except the cross. All of his personal agendas, prior to the cross, were irrelevant now. His past didn't matter now. The only thing left for a man condemned to the cross was what lay ahead—the unavoidable cross!

Jesus didn't hesitate when it came to describing discipleship in His kingdom and used what was perhaps the most negative metaphor imaginable to the first-century mind: death by crucifixion. If those who first heard Him speak those words were alarmed and confused, they would better understand when Jesus Himself died on a cross. Following Jesus meant abandoning everything else as if it did not exist in order to follow Jesus. His followers "die" to everything else, including their own lives, if they are to follow Him.

As a metaphor for the Christian life, nothing could be clearer than the picture of the cross. When we surrender our lives to Christ, we give up our personal agendas and passions and surrender our past, present, and future to Christ. The cross demonstrates not only a surrendered life but also a spiritually tough life. No matter what the demonic enemy or worldly circumstances throw at us, the Christian endures. The Christian who takes up the cross is already dead to the interests of the world: its temptations, its ridicule, its man-made philosophies, and whatever else is opposed to Christ. The only thing that matters for the surrendered believer is the will of God. No wonder Paul said, "But far be it from me to boast except in the cross of our Lord Jesus Christ, by which the world has been crucified to me, and I to the world" (Gal. 6:14). For the believer carrying a cross, the world has lost its hold on his heart, and the world's pull on the flesh—its attraction—is diminished.

How can a human being with all of his idiosyncrasies, failures, and self-interests live a "crucified life"? We are accustomed to the pleasures and pains of this life from the time of childhood. How can we carry a cross when our sense of self-preservation is so intense? What did Jesus say?

Decide (v. 23)

Jesus knew the power of temptation. He was tempted by all the things that tempt us (Heb. 4:15). In addition, not only did Jesus experience temptation (yet without sin); He has watched all of us fail time and again throughout life. So note carefully the words of Jesus, "If anyone would come after me. . . ." The word for "would" is the word meaning "wish" or "will." In other words, it takes a desire to follow Christ. No one is likely to endure the life that requires a cross if he hasn't decided for himself to follow. An inherited religion, one merely accepted as a matter of tradition, can be shallow and detached. The life Jesus calls us to live is passionate and personal. The disciple who bears a cross is willing to die for his faith if called upon because he is committed to Christ in a decisive and personal way. Apart from that personal desire, the temptations that face the follower of Jesus would not only overwhelm; they would eventually wear an uncommitted individual to fatigue and failure. While no surrendered follower of Christ can honestly take any credit for spiritual progress, without a desire to remain faithful, spiritual failure is assured.

Daily (v. 23)

The fastest animal on earth is the cheetah. It can hit speeds of seventy-five miles per hour, but those speeds only endure briefly. Life is like that in some ways. We often lack the endurance to keep our commitments in full. Jesus understood His followers. He understands that, like the cheetah, we have to start over on a regular basis if we are to keep our commitment. Therefore, Jesus encourages us to take up our cross—to surrender our lives to His will—on a daily basis.

For example, one important key to living the Christian life is the insistence of Jesus that His followers demonstrate faithfulness. We have an illustration of that principle in the experience of the leader of the early church. Peter failed Jesus by betraying Him the night of His arrest. After His resurrection, almost immediately, Jesus reinstated the inconsistent follower (John 18:25–27; John 21:4–19). In the kingdom of Jesus, beginning again is fundamental to the movement. His followers have to live with the freedom and responsibility to start again each day. Peter's failure and reinstatement exemplifies what Jesus meant by carrying the cross daily. The Christian life starts over each day regardless of the success or failure of the previous day. Is that what Paul meant when he said, "Brothers, I do not consider that I have made it my own. But one thing I do: forgetting what lies behind and straining forward to what lies ahead, I press on toward the goal for the prize of the upward call of God in Christ Jesus" (Phil. 3:13–14).

Deny (v. 23)

As I write these words, I am in Jerusalem where I visited Yad Vishem, the Holocaust Museum. An emotional statue at the Children's Memorial shows Janusz Korczak and a group of frightened Jewish children headed to the gas chamber. Our guide explained that Korczak operated an orphanage in Poland. When the children were ordered to their deaths by the Nazis, Korczak was offered freedom, but he refused to leave his children. He voluntarily stayed with them, and they were all killed in the gas chamber. His life was a portrait of self-denial. He set aside his desire for life in order to comfort children who were forced to die. In order to comfort them, he gave up comfort for himself.

When Jesus told His disciples they had to deny themselves, He used a word which means "to repudiate" self. The word in verse 23, translated "deny," literally means "to deny knowing a person." Taking up a cross means self-interest has to be denied, personal desire has to be abandoned. Like Janusz Korczak, who denied himself for the sake of others, taking up a cross, by its definition, is a lifestyle of self-denial for the sake of following Christ. While we may initially react negatively to the extreme demands of discipleship, the call for self-denial is, after all, an invitation from Jesus Himself and cannot be ignored.

Have you considered the Lord's invitation to take up a cross? If you pick up the cross and follow Christ, you will be living the life He has planned for you, and you will discover a life you never imagined (v. 24). His agenda will become your agenda, and His lifestyle will increasingly become your lifestyle. You will be more than a nominal Christian or a casual observer. You will be a disciple of the fourth cross.

For Memory and Meditation

"And he said to all, 'If anyone would come after me, let him deny himself and take up his cross daily and follow me.'" Luke 9:23

------

[1] Rob Phillips, "Call to Prayer: The Persecuted Church," Baptist Press, www.bpnews.net/BPFirstPerson.asp?id=41401, accessed November 1, 2013.

[2] John R. W. Stott, *The Cross of Christ* (Downers Grove, IL: InterVarsity Press, 1986), 23.

That One Big Thing
Focal Text: Mark 12:28–34

WEEK 9

It was all decided. They had crossed the point of no return. Jesus had to go.

What started as a theological difference was now deeply personal; they hated Him with an irrational, boiling passion. As a result, the desire to kill Jesus had reached a fever pitch. If the assassination attempts had been impromptu and uncoordinated in the beginning, they were orchestrated and premeditated now (Luke 4:28–30). The problem facing them was His popularity among the uneducated crowds. He was a hero to the majority of the people, and any attempt to stop Him might backfire. They needed a foolproof plan.

For years the rabbis had created theological arguments that almost no one could answer, biblical Gordian knots that could tangle up the brightest young rabbinical students. Why not trap Him with one of those? If they could catch Him in an unguarded contradiction or a biblical slip of any kind, His credibility would be publicly damaged, the crowds would lose interest in Him, and that would make it easier to get rid of Him. What they needed now was a "gotcha" moment. So they developed their list of questions that, if answered incorrectly, would, at the very least, insult the untrained crowds that surrounded Him.

They planned their attack with military precision, as if they were taking a city with waves of assault. They sent in one inquisitor after another. No one, they reasoned, would be able to withstand the onslaught. If He survived the first round, they would wear Him down with the second, the third, or the fourth. They had Him now; they were certain of it. They would simply overwhelm Him with a deluge of difficult trick questions designed to trip Him up in front of His gullible followers. It was only a matter of time before their theological "shock and awe" would win the day!

Their perfect plan had only one flaw: Jesus of Nazareth was more than ready for them.

Round 1: Taxes
Mark 12:13–17

Who likes paying taxes? If anyone did, it wasn't the average workingman in Israel. After all, he was barely earning enough in a day to meet the needs of that day. To make things worse, he was paying taxes to a regime that denied Israel the right to its own sovereignty. Rome was the enemy. The grumbling, public sentiment about taxes was clear.

The dilemma was obvious. If Jesus was asked about taxes paid to Rome and took the popular view that they were unfair, then the religious authorities could accuse Him of rabble-rousing against Rome. On the other hand, if Jesus sided with Rome and advocated paying taxes, the crowds would turn on Him in an instant. Either way, the theologians reasoned, they had Jesus on the horns of a dilemma. There was no right answer.

Jesus knew a hypocrite when He saw one (v. 15) so He had them produce a Roman coin with Caesar's image engraved on it: "And they brought one. And he said to them, 'Whose likeness and inscription is this?' They said to him, 'Caesar's.' Jesus said to them, 'Render to Caesar the things that are Caesar's, and to God the things that are God's.' And they marveled at him" (Mark 12:16–17). He easily backed them into an unexpected corner. Round one went to Jesus.

Round 2: Marriage, Death, and the Afterlife
Mark 12:18–27

The Sadducees were a small sect of religious leaders who held enormous sway over the lives of the Jews of Jesus' day. They represented only about 1 percent of the total population, but their influence was out of proportion to their relatively small numbers because they controlled the ministry of the temple and were the political representatives of the Jews to the Roman government.

After Jesus had easily dismissed the attempted ambush of the rival religious leaders among the Pharisees, the Sadducees stepped up with their trap. The Sadducees went straight to the point: Jewish law insisted men had the responsibility of marrying the widow of their deceased brother in order to care for her and continue the dead brother's name among the family tree (see the book of Ruth). The Sadducees, who did not believe in an afterlife, had no doubt confused numerous opponents in the past with their outrageous tale of one woman who had been the wife of seven brothers in a row who each died. How, they wondered, would there be peace in heaven since all the Jewish brothers would be there with only the one wife? It was an awkward thought to say the least.

What would Jesus say? The common people believed in heaven, but no one wanted eternity populated with a few wives sharing multiple husbands! Would Jesus disagree with the Bible or with Jewish tradition? Would He concede that there would be no heaven? It was a clever argument.

As usual Jesus was both original and practical while affirming the integrity of the Scripture. He bluntly told them they were wrong because they didn't understand Scripture (what a charge to level at the leaders of the Jewish temple!) and they had an anemic view of the power of God. In heaven, Jesus informed them, no one is married since marriage ends at death (vv. 24–25). The Sadducees were stunned into silence. Jesus' answer was so simple. The people standing nearby must have wondered why no one had realized it before. If the Pharisees and Sadducees were trying to diminish the credibility and popularity of Jesus, they were failing miserably. He was looking better than ever!

Round 3: The Big, Right Question
Mark 12:28–34

When the California pastor Rick Warren wrote *The Purpose Driven Life*, it sold millions of copies, making it one of the biggest selling books in history. The explanations for its success may be numerous, but one reason stands out as the most obvious: the subject of the book struck a chord with a culture in search of life's meaning. What is our purpose? What does God want from us? Why are we here? The final question posed to Jesus touched on the subject of life's meaning and God's purpose for our lives. It is, after all, the big question.

Unlike the previous questioners, the Bible teacher who asked the big question seemed more sincere. This last question came from the heart. He had thought about his question long before he met Jesus. He had probably debated it with other sincere scholars many times. He had never arrived at a satisfactory answer. Since Jesus seemed to know how to solve complex problems so impressively, the teacher of the law posed the biggest question he had ever considered: Which commandment is the most important of all? (Mark 12:28).

For a twenty-first-century reader a question about Hebrew commandments may not seem to be the biggest question of all. After closer analysis, however, we realize that ancient question is the main issue of life.

It isn't hard to see why the people wanted clarification concerning the list of laws. There were 613 Jewish commandments, and scholars had speculated that there might be one of more importance than all the others. What it might be had been the subject of endless debate.

Not surprisingly Jesus had thought about it too. He had an answer. In His response we can find the clues needed to solve the main mystery of our lives: What is my life all about?

Love God
Mark 12:29–30
Jesus quoted many Scriptures. Nearly eighty times in the Gospels Jesus quoted a specific reference from the Old Testament. His words are so steeped in Old Testament allusions, it is virtually impossible to assign a number to the times His words reflect an Old Testament passage. When asked about the "most important commandment," Jesus, as usual, turned to the Bible for the answer.

To the Jewish scribe, a man immersed in the study of the Bible, the question about the most important commandment was another way of asking, "What is the one most important thing in life?" Jesus wasted no time in providing the answer. Loving God is the most important thing in life.

The command Jesus singled out as the greatest (the Greek word is *protos* and means "first in priority") comes from Deuteronomy 6:4–5 and is referred to as the Shema. The Jewish scribe, like every other Jewish man, would have been extremely familiar with the Shema and would have likely quoted it that very morning and every other morning as the centerpiece of his daily prayers.

Jesus insisted that loving God is an all-encompassing commitment involving every aspect of a disciple's life. He used four words to describe the priority of loving God.

Jesus said the disciple should love God with all of his heart. The Greek word *kardia*, from which we get our words *cardiac* and *cardiology*, refers to the emotional center of life. The reason the heart is associated with emotion should be obvious. Our emotions affect the heart rate and we feel it. Loving God is an emotional issue.

Next, He said we should love God with all of our soul. The word "soul" is the Greek word *psyche* and comes from a root word meaning "the breath of life." We might say the soul is the force of life within us. It is our inner being. So Jesus teaches us that loving God is a spiritual devotion springing from the depths of our spiritual, inner being. It is a love that goes as deep as we can imagine, as deep as our own awareness.

Jesus also said we should love God with our entire mind. This aspect of loving God would have been clear to the scribe. He spent his life studying. Loving God with the mind means we think about Him and devote the power of intelligence not only to studying about God but also to knowing God. The ultimate goal of loving God with our mind is knowing God.

He also reminded the scribe that disciples must love God with their strength. For those tempted to live a merely contemplative life, Jesus rouses them to a life of action. He calls us to love God with our bodies, our actions, and our physical abilities. Jesus would later send His followers into the world for evangelism and missions. He needed those followers to be activists! Loving God requires us to break a sweat.

In summary, Jesus expects us to love God emotionally, spiritually, intellectually, and physically! Loving God is a verb and functions as a command. In addition, in order to understand the depth of loving God, we have to reflect on the repetition of the word "all": *all* of our heart, soul, mind, and strength. Loving God is priority one!

Love Others
Mark 12:31–32

The scribe was impressed with both Jesus and himself because the Shema was already his daily prayer and he had memorized it from childhood. Jesus, however, wasn't through and answered a question the scribe hadn't asked: "What is the second most important commandment?" Remember, the scribe appears to be part of the delegation sent to trap Jesus in His own words. While listening to Jesus debate the others, the scribe became fascinated with the Lord's answers and had an apparent change of heart (v. 28). Jesus knew that and pressed deeper than the scribe was initially willing to go. Loving God is primary, but loving our neighbor is important too (v. 31).

From Jesus' point of view, loving God and loving other people are inseparable actions. The scribe and his friends failed at both, and the second failure most clearly proved the first. If the scribe had loved people, he would not have been in a conspiracy to trap Jesus in the first place! Jesus confronted the scribe with his greatest failing: he claimed to love God, but he did not love other people. Jesus reminded the scribe of the heart of Leviticus 19:18, "But you shall love your neighbor as yourself: I am the Lord."

The command to love others is not a sentimental afterthought. Jesus commands us to love our neighbor with the same intensity and consistency with which we love ourselves. It is a radical worldview!

In light of the priority of loving God and people, we ought to ask, "Where has this lifestyle ever been tried, and how did it work?" The answer to that question is the life of Jesus Himself. He loved God with everything in Him, and He loved us as much as He loved Himself. The early church did the same (Acts 2:42–47). In both cases where it was tried, it worked miraculously well. The answer to life's most important question is direct: love God and love people. Now, what will you do with that one big question?

For Memory and Meditation

"And you shall love the Lord your God with all your heart and with all your soul and with all you mind and with all your strength." Mark 12:30

With Jesus in the Garden of Broken Hearts

Focal Text: Matthew 26:36–46

He came home one day and his wife had taken their son and moved in with another man. He didn't see it coming. He was devastated.

A fire started in the mobile home where a single mom lived with her two children. The fire was on the other side of the mobile home where the children were sleeping. Her neighbors got her out but the children were lost. Her pain was unimaginable.

The father and son didn't see eye to eye on anything. One day in the late 1960s the long-haired son let the screen door to his father's house slam hard behind him as he stormed out after an argument with his father. That was more than forty years ago, and an aged, tormented father wonders every day if his son will ever come back because he never heard from him again.

They seemed like a match made in heaven. He left for college and expected her to wait, but she met someone else and got married while he was gone. He never got over it.

He had loved her for more than sixty years of marriage. When she died, he was crushed. His funeral followed hers by only a few weeks. His family said he died of a broken heart.

Their son was a young dad with a beautiful, loving wife and baby, but he was killed by a drunk driver one day not far from home. Those parents were never the same.

These are all real stories of real people—I knew them all. Their testimonies of crushing emotional pain represent only a few of the heartbroken people we all know.

Joseph Parker knew about a broken heart. He was the pastor of City Temple in nineteenth-century Victorian London during the Golden Age of British Christianity. Every Sunday he preached to thousands of people. His books were sold around the world. His church building was an architectural marvel of the time. Joseph Parker was celebrated and successful, and yet he had a broken heart. His first wife died when he was a young pastor after twelve happy years of marriage. He married a second time, and she also died. Some say he never got over it.[1] Knowing the background of his experience, one of his most famous statements takes on a richer, deeper tone. While teaching younger ministers, he offered this advice: "Preach to the suffering and you will never lack a congregation. There is a broken heart in every pew."[2]

Have you ever suffered from a broken heart? Like so many others, perhaps you, too, have stood beside the grave while the casket of the one you loved was lowered into the earth. In that moment you may have felt as if your dreams, your life, and all your tomorrows were being lowered into the grave with the coffin. Or perhaps someone has walked out on you or betrayed you. Maybe your hopes for a career were ended by an accident or an illness. The possible ways we could be hurt are nearly endless. Life, we've learned by now, is fragile. Perhaps at our lowest points we have all wondered, "Does God know how I feel? Does He care about me?"

In the Garden Alone
Matthew 26:36–38

The life of Jesus may be the most studied and the most misunderstood of any life ever lived. In one of the most unexpected scenes from His life, we find Him alone in the dark, begging to avoid the very thing He had repeatedly predicted would happen. His heart is broken, His time is short, His prayers are desperate, and in many ways He has never seemed more like one of us than in those terrible hours in the garden of Gethsemane.

In the upper room He had been confident and focused. Now in the garden, a few hours later, He is vulnerable and emotional and asking for support.

The garden of Gethsemane was an impressive grove of olive trees on the western slope of the Mount of Olives. The word *Gethsemane* means "olive press." The name itself serves as an important metaphor for the most memorable events that took place in its shadows the night Jesus was betrayed. He and the disciples may have camped there during the week of Passover since Jerusalem was filled with Jewish pilgrims who had flooded the city for the festival. Many of them would have chosen the Mount of Olives as the perfect place to camp after their long journeys. It is close to Jerusalem and, therefore, the temple, which would have been clearly visible from the garden. In any event, after the traditional Passover meal Jesus and His followers walked the steep hillside down from Jerusalem, across the Kidron Valley, up the sharp, inclined slope of the Mount of Olives to the garden. There Jesus split His disciples into two groups.

After separating the groups, Jesus invited His inner circle of three friends to follow Him deeper into the darkness of the olive groves. Apparently He wanted privacy even from the other eight disciples (Judas had already left the group). To the three who had also accompanied Him up to the Mount of Transfiguration (Matt. 17:1–9) and to the raising of the dead girl to life (Mark 5:37–42), Jesus added the request that they join Him for a private prayer retreat in the garden of Gethsemane.

Jesus had a lot on His mind that night. He was fully aware of the plot to assassinate Him. In fact, He barely talked of anything else in the days leading up to that night. A few days earlier, for instance, He stated categorically that He would be killed during the Passover, and then at a dinner party in Bethany, He spoke openly of His burial (Matt. 26:1, 12). While with His disciples for the Passover meal, He surprised them with the prediction that one of them would betray Him (Matt. 26:20–25). As He shared the unleavened bread of the meal, He said it was His body that would be broken, and the cup during the meal that night He likened to His own shed blood (Matt. 26: 26, 28).

Now the time had nearly come, and the emotional pressure was intense and taking its toll. As He walked deeper into the darkness of the grove, He confided to His three close friends—Peter, James, and John—that He was deeply sad and overcome with a dreadful sense of grief (v. 37). The feeling was intense depression (v. 37). The word "troubled" comes from a root meaning "to loathe" and is one of the strongest Greek words to describe emotional distress or depression. The feeling was so dark and foreboding, so heavy and unmanageable; Jesus said He felt as if He was dying on the inside (v. 38).

Have you ever experienced the shadows of emotional depression? It may be hard to imagine it if you have only seen Jesus portrayed as a kind of cheerful, positive, passive mystic, but Jesus experienced an intense depression the night He was betrayed. The twisted contortions of olive trees cast eerie shadows at night with only the light of the moon above them. In that grove of trees, known as the place of "the olive press," Jesus experienced a broken heart. He was in the vise grip of emotional pressure so heavy He could barely endure it. In the garden of the olive press, He was in a psychological "press." The New International Version captures the spiritual torture of that hour when it quotes Jesus saying, "My soul is overwhelmed with sorrow to the point of death" (v. 38). There in the quiet darkness, where the only sounds were those natural to the deep of the night, Jesus pierced the silence with crying and praying in the guttural laments of the Aramaic language.

What event, what loss, what disappointment has driven you to the point of despair? Have you ever hurt so deeply that you fell into an emotional numbness from the sorrow and the unrelenting harshness of emotional heartbreak? Maybe your business failed or you lost your job or your home. Maybe you felt the sting of losing the one person you thought would never leave you. Perhaps your child was in the hospital and the prognosis was grim. Maybe the marriage of your dreams became a nightmare of betrayals. No matter what left you emotionally wounded and scarred with pain you never knew existed, Jesus knows how you feel. He has been there, too.

Why the Pain?
Matthew 26:39–44

"Let this cup pass from me" (v. 39). This may be, prior to the cross, the most agonizing prayer ever prayed. Jesus left the inner circle of His three close friends and went into the shadows, perhaps to avoid any additional scrutiny while He cried and prayed (vv. 38–39). Once comfortably away from the remaining eleven disciples, Jesus fell, as if exhausted or fatigued to the point of collapse, facedown on the ground and started to pray. The wording leaves little doubt about the intensity of the scene. Jesus "fell" facedown to the ground (v. 39). He did not casually sit down for prayer. He collapsed, as if pushed or unable to continue standing, due to some great weight or burden He was carrying. It is the only time in the New Testament we find Jesus in this posture. When considered along with the other descriptions of His emotional stability that night, a composite comes together revealing a man with a broken heart and a tortured soul. How is this possible? Is this the Jesus you thought you knew? Why was He in such agony?

Speculation is unhelpful. His own words tell the story. Three times He prayed about avoiding a "cup" that He was being led to drink (vv. 38–44). That "cup" was the source of His dread and His emotional distress. What was the "cup"? On one level, of course, He dreaded the physical aspects of death on a cross. Filmmakers, historical art, and well-intentioned contemporary sermons focus much more on the brutality of the cross than the actual descriptions in the New Testament, which are all surprisingly discreet (Matt. 27:35; Mark 15:24–25; Luke 23:33; John 19:18). Naturally, as a young man Jesus did not look forward to the harsh cruelty of the crucifixion. But the "cup" was much more than the physical suffering and an even more painful reality than the Roman nails that pinned His body to the cross.

The New Testament insists Jesus went to the cross to pay the price for sin and take upon Himself the wrath of God against sin and to experience it in a more frightening and personal way than we usually consider (2 Cor. 5:21; Heb. 2:9). The Oxford scholar Michael Green best captures the sense of it in his blunt assessment of what happened in the garden: "He tasted the hell of separation from God the Father as He hung upon that cross. And in the garden He got the first, bitter taste of what our salvation was going to cost."[3] The "cup" Jesus dreaded so intensely was that of enduring the wrath of God against our sin. What He experienced in the garden was a premonition of how dreadful that experience would be. It is, I think, impossible for us to appreciate fully the depths of hell He endured on the cross. Even more incomprehensible is the fact that the sin He suffered for was mine and not His.

Responding to Emotional Pain
Matthew 26:37–44

If you have been trained to see the Christian life as one perpetual high, the experience of Jesus in the garden must be hard to process. Denying the emptiness that sometimes defines our experience in life does nothing to heal the hollow places created by the stabbing of emotional pain. We will experience mind-numbing pain in life at times, and when we do, we need to know how to handle it. In those forsaken hours when we venture into the "garden of broken hearts" in our own lives, we can turn to the experience of Jesus and what He did to endure the pain to find healing for our own.

First, remember, Jesus prayed. Even in His deepest depression He prayed, "My Father, if it be possible, let this cup pass from me" (v. 39). Notice the intimacy of the prayer: "My Father." Jesus still knew whom to trust when His heart was broken! Next we notice Jesus relied on His personal prayer partners! He invited the disciples to "watch with me" (v. 38), which clearly meant prayer since He asked them an hour later, "Could you not watch with me one hour? Watch and pray" (vv. 38, 40–41). Each of us should cultivate a small group of trusted friends who can come to our side in prayer and support, no matter how inconvenient it may be for them at the moment. In addition, we should be that kind of praying friend for a small group of others.

We will not be able to live full lives and, at the same time, avoid the "garden of broken hearts," but we can learn to pray, "Not as I will, but as you will" (v. 39). In communion with Christ, we will discover a strength to face the emotional pain of life, and we, too, will survive the heartbreak of the cross so we can enjoy the celebration of eventual resurrection.

For Memory and Meditation

"And going a little farther he fell on his face and prayed, saying, 'My Father, if it be possible, let this cup pass from me; nevertheless, not as I will, but as you will.'" Matthew 26:39

---

[1] Hugh Chisolm, ed. (1911) "Parker, Joseph," Encyclopedia Britannica (11th ed.) Cambridge University Press in Wikipedia, en.wikipedia.org/wiki/Joseph_Parker_(theologian), accessed March 19, 2014.

[2] Chuck Swindoll, The Pastor's Blog Encouraging Words for Pastors, www.insightforliving.typepad.com/insightforliving-blog/2014/01/to help you counsel, accessed March 19, 2014.

[3] Michael Green, *The Message of Matthew* (Downers Grove, IL: InterVarsity Press, 1988, 2000), 280.

The Day Jesus Died
Focal Text: Luke 23:1–49

It is impossible to understand Jesus apart from His death on the cross. No matter how many cultures He is introduced into or how many centuries have passed since He lived, He is recognized everywhere by how He died. For instance, today, as I write these words twenty centuries after the event, a book called *Killing Jesus* is on The New York Times Best Sellers List, where it has been for twenty-four weeks at the time of this writing.[1]

Obviously, the cross still fascinates the postmodern mind. Even some who doubt the historical integrity of the New Testament concede that the death of Jesus occurred and helped give rise to the movement that bears His name. For example, Robert Funk, the founder of The Jesus Seminar, writes that the body of Jesus may have rotted on the cross becoming food for wild dogs and birds. He adds that his colleagues on The Jesus Seminar reluctantly think it might be possible Jesus was buried, but they are thoroughly convinced that if He was buried, His grave, along with His decomposing body, was soon forgotten. Yet, in spite of his blatant dismissal of orthodox belief about the resurrection of Jesus, he admits that the evidence shows Jesus was in fact crucified in Jerusalem during the reign of Pontius Pilate while the Jews were celebrating Passover.[2] Funk, who dryly rejects the possibility of the deity of Jesus and believes instead that He was a poet (thereby rejecting the miracle of the incarnation and the supernatural claim of the resurrection), is, nonetheless, left with the naked fact of a cross planted boldly in the unavoidable center of the story of Jesus of Nazareth.[3]

Why is the cross so conspicuous in the biography of Jesus Christ? Why does the New Testament focus so much attention on the death of Jesus? Why, after two thousand years, is the cross still the universal sign of global Christianity? Why do our songwriters keep giving us new songs to sing about the cross? Why do churches name themselves after the instrument of our founder's death? Why do we decorate our buildings with the cross? Why do we wear the cross as meaningful and treasured jewelry? Why do we keep writing books, painting pictures, and preaching sermons about the death of an Israeli carpenter turned preacher who lived two thousand years ago? What is it, after all, that is so magnetic about the cross?

In the case of most people, death is virtually the end of their story. A few individuals may be remembered, but their personal contribution to life ends at death. Not so with Jesus—His death essentially makes His story come alive! It seems the prophecy Jesus made about His own death has been and continues to be fulfilled repeatedly in every generation for two thousand years in cities, villages, families, and tribes all over the world. Regarding His own death by crucifixion, He predicted, "And I, when I am lifted up from the earth, will draw all people to myself" (John 12:32). He wasn't talking about "lifting" Himself up in praise, preaching, or prayer. He was speaking about the physical, historical event when He was lifted up on the cross to die! That's the event that draws the world to Him (John 12:33).

What really happened the day Jesus died? Why does it still matter so much?

Not Guilty!
Luke 23:1–25

The amount of detail devoted to the last days of Jesus has been called "disproportionate" to the rest of the story of His life, due to the fact that between one-fourth and one-third of the first three Gospels are devoted to His death and the last week of life leading up to the cross. John's Gospel appears to be divided almost in half with the last half devoted to the "passion"—that is, the last few days of Jesus' life on earth, including the crucifixion.[4] Clearly the cross is central to the biblical understanding of Jesus. Even His first four biographers were unquestionably fixated on that one event.

In that last week of His life, when Jesus arrived in Jerusalem for the Passover celebration, the city was filled with spiritual pilgrims from around Israel and throughout the world, since Passover was the most important feast on the Jewish calendar. After a week of public ministry in the busy city of Jerusalem, Jesus was betrayed by one of His followers, arrested late one night, and was "tried" in the bloodthirsty spirit of mob rule by the religious leaders in an impromptu "trial" at dawn. In a cold, cruelly ironic twist, they were in a hurry because they did not want the execution of Jesus to interfere with their religious duties later in the day!

Once they had a consensus that Jesus was guilty of a capital offense, they took Him to a civil magistrate, Pilate, the anti-Semitic Roman governor of Judea. The religious leaders demanded that Jesus be crucified, but after questioning Jesus, Pilate repeatedly attempted to excuse the unusually subdued prisoner and absolve Him of any legal wrongdoing. In spite of the furious and overzealous demands of the religious leaders, at least four times Pilate, the Roman leader and the only one with the authority to condemn Jesus to death, stated that he could find no guilt in Jesus at all (Luke 23:4, 14–15, 20–22). Even Herod (the son of Herod the Great, the murderous king reigning when Jesus was born), the Galilean ruler during most of Jesus' lifetime, found no justifiable reason to crucify Jesus when given the opportunity (vv. 7–11).

When searching for the reason Jesus died, whatever else might be said, it cannot be claimed He was a threat to Rome. The civil authorities ridiculed Him, underestimated Him, and dismissed Him, but they did not want to crucify Him!

The Cross
Luke 23:26–38

While Pilate did not want to crucify Jesus, and famously "washed his hands" (Matt. 27:24) of the entire matter (at least in his own mind), he did eventually cave to the pressure of the priests and other religious leaders. He had Jesus savagely beaten to the point that He was barely recognizable and then sent Him to a place called "The Skull" to be crucified with common criminals.

It was a long walk to the crucifixion site, considering the blood loss, exposure, physical lacerations, and pain from the beating Jesus was already experiencing. In addition to the Roman flogging, He had been punched in the face repeatedly by Roman soldiers (John 18:22), the most formidable fighting force in the world at the time, and by the religious leaders, who had been whipped into a frenzied bloodlust at the thought of finally ridding the world of Jesus

(Matt. 26:67–68). As a result of the exhaustion and abuse He had already endured, the heavy cross He was forced to carry proved to be too much, and Jesus stumbled under its weight. As a result, a Libyan Jew named Simon of Cyrene was randomly snatched from the crowd of onlookers and compelled into service to carry the cross of Jesus.

The Skull, or Golgotha in Hebrew, was a place known for crucifixion and associated with death and thus the name. It might have also received the name from an outcrop of jagged stone near the street shaped like a human skull. It was an eerie place with a terrible name and the stench of death, no matter what the reason for its moniker. Once there Jesus was immediately stripped, and the soldiers, unconcerned with another Jewish crucifixion, jumped at the chance to gamble for His clothes in an unplanned game of chance. They had no way of knowing it, but by doing so, they were fulfilling an ancient messianic prophecy (Ps. 22:16–18).

In spite of the cruelty of the cross, the Gospel writers are unusually restrained in describing what happened. Instead of going into graphic detail, Luke merely says, "They crucified Him" (v. 33). There is no mention of the appearance of the cross. Nails are not mentioned. Luke even leaves out any mention of the blood. The apostles would later find great significance in the blood (Acts 20:28; Eph. 1:7; Col. 1:20; Heb. 9:14; 1 Pet. 1:2; 1 John 1:7; Rev. 1:5, etc.); and Jesus mentioned it at the Last Supper, but on the day of the crucifixion itself, descriptive words were few.

The words that were in abundance were criticisms hurled at Jesus while He hung on the cross. A careful study of the four Gospels reveals the most frequently said thing to Jesus while He was dying on the cross was "save yourself." In Luke's account alone we find at least three individuals or groups taunting Jesus to save Himself. The religious leaders mocked Him as He suffered and implored Him to save Himself (v. 35). The soldiers said the same thing (v. 37). Finally one of the criminals chided Him to save Himself (v. 39). These aggravating taunts also fulfilled Scripture (Ps. 22: 6–8)! But Jesus did not go to the cross to save Himself. He went to the cross to save us!

When searching for clues about why Jesus died, the fulfillment of Old Testament prophecy helps us grasp the shocking answer to the mystery—Jesus went to the cross because it was the will of God (Isa. 53:4–6). The New Testament witness is consistent—the death of Jesus on the cross provides payment for sin, allows us to experience forgiveness, and pays the price for our salvation.

Last Words
Luke 23:39–43
Only Luke records a brief conversation between Jesus and the two men on crosses on either side of Him. Talking would have been difficult, and at times impossible, due to the excruciating pain of the cross. In addition, the victim was hanging with his arms stretched out; and when he sagged on the cross from his own weight, his rib cage pressed down on his lungs. Each breath and each word required him to pull up to exhale and inhale. This process actually hastened death, as the victim would finally grow exhausted from the decreased oxygen in his blood and the tearing pain of his weight supported by long nails holding him to the cross.

Not much is known about the identity of the other two men hanging there except what the Bible tells us. The English word "criminals" (vv. 32, 33, 39), which describes the men, is literally the phrase "workers of evil" or "wicked workers." Apparently this description is apt because one of them admitted they both deserved the death penalty (v. 40). They were obviously guilty of terrible crimes and not merely political prisoners.

One of the men was harassing Jesus to work a miracle and save them all from death on the cross, if He was really who He claimed to be. His interest was not spiritual; He was working one last angle to avoid the death penalty! But the other man suddenly realized the condition He was in and who was hanging near Him. Perhaps he looked up at the inscription written above Jesus, "King of the Jews," and recognized that his only hope was in forgiveness. Regardless of what struck a chord of repentance in his heart, he confessed his guilt and humbly asked to be remembered when Jesus entered His kingdom. It was a simple request; yet it demonstrated tremendous faith! He was dying and so was Jesus. Jesus had been so savagely beaten that He looked like raw meat hanging on the cross. In fact, His life was almost over. Yet, to the repentant criminal, Jesus looked like a King!

To the dying man, Jesus offered a promise that tells us something about the Lord Himself. He told the guilty prisoner that after death he would be with Christ in paradise (v. 43)! What does it tell us about Jesus that He was willing to look no deeper into the man's background than his request for mercy? Jesus granted his simple request and more. He promised the guilty man forgiveness, salvation, and eternal life. The man's prayer was uninformed and childlike. It wasn't theologically rich or lengthy. Some might even be tempted to argue it was too ambiguous to adequately represent saving faith. But Jesus heard the man's prayer, and that is all that matters.

In that dying thief's final prayer we discover the real significance of the cross! Jesus came to save sinners—even those who pray unimpressive prayers and have only enough life left to humbly cry, "Remember me!" Even those sinners who have done the worst things in life—even the ones society correctly judges, incarcerates, or condemns—can be forgiven and saved because Jesus died for sinners. The cross of Jesus was the throne of His new kingdom, and the criminal was one of the first subjects of the kingdom to recognize the King. Even today the cross shouts over the clamor of guilty consciences, the noise of self-justifying excuses, and the rumbling thunder of personal, moral failures. After all these years it still holds out this promise: "You can find mercy." To those who have gone too far or sinned on an epic scale or allowed themselves to travel down a road marked "no exit," the cross has a message: "You, too, can be saved!"

For Memory and Meditation
"And he said to him, 'Truly, I say to you, today you will be with me in Paradise.'" Luke 23:43

---

[1] www.nytimes.com/best-sellers-books/2014-03-23/hardcover-nonfiction/list.html, accessed March 19, 2014.

[2] Robert W. Funk, *Honest to Jesus* (San Francisco, CA: HarpersCollins, A Polebridge Press Book, 1996), 219–21.

[3] Ibid., 2.

[4] John R. W. Stott, *The Cross of Christ* (Downers Grove, IL, InterVarsity Press, 1986), 32.

Jesus Is Alive!

Focal Text: Luke 24:36–49

First he was dead. Then he wasn't dead. He didn't even know he was dead until text messages started piling up from family and friends checking on his health. Quinton Ross was home in Texas when the *New York Post* reported the former NBA player, who finished his NBA career with the New Jersey Nets, had been killed, stuffed in a trash bag, and buried on a beach in New York. Family and friends were panicked when they could not immediately reach Ross by phone. After receiving so many text messages, he went on the Internet and read that he was dead. The paper retracted the erroneous story but not before sending family members and friends of the former NBA player into shock, grief, and disbelief. "They were saying I was dead," Ross said. "It was a tough day, mostly for my family and friends."[1]

Have you ever received news of a friend's death only to learn later the report was incorrect? It happened to me once. I was told a good friend of mine had died. I was shocked and saddened. Fortunately it wasn't true. I was thrilled to learn he was still alive, but I was also confused about how the news of his death got so convoluted in the first place. In the case of the basketball player and in my friend's case, it was all a mistake. As Mark Twain once quipped, "The reports of my death have been greatly exaggerated!" But what if your friend was actually dead and buried? If he came back to life after that, how would you feel? How would you intellectually process that unprecedented event?

That is exactly what happened to the apostles and other followers of Jesus. He was brutally killed. Then He was alive again. It was so shocking to see Him after He rose from the dead; they thought they were seeing an apparition or a ghost! They could not believe what they were seeing and hearing as He greeted them that first day (Luke 24:37–41).

Alive Again
Luke 24:39–43

Since so many years have passed since the resurrection occurred, how can we be certain it took place at all? After all, there were no cameras to record the event. There are no medical records to confirm either the death or the resurrection. How can we know it really happened? What evidence exists?

Jesus was quick to anticipate that question since He would appear in bodily form to relatively few people. Immediately when He appeared to His surprised disciples, He began establishing the nature of the resurrection as an actual event that took place in the same way other actual events in life occur, such as eating, touching, seeing, and hearing. In this way He started the process of convincing the world that He had conquered death by first convincing a few reliable eyewitnesses. He spoke to the group audibly (v. 38). One person might be accused of hearing things, but it would be virtually impossible and strains credibility to accuse an entire group of hearing the same auditory hallucinations. They each heard His audible voice and His intelligent sentences telling them all the same thing. Throughout the rest of their lives, they never wavered from that testimony (2 Pet. 1:16; 1 John 1:1).

Jesus physically appeared to the entire group, and they all saw Him. He wasn't a vision or a dream. They saw Him in the same way they saw the rest of the world around them. He requested that they examine His wounds for themselves, which He had received as a result of the crucifixion. He was insistent they actually touch His body, feel the texture of His flesh, and acknowledge the firmness of His skeletal structure (vv. 39–40). He wasn't an apparition or a spirit or a vision; Jesus appeared to them as a man. Then He went further. He ate in their presence. He was no phantasm. He was real, and He consumed His lunch as they observed in stunned silence and gleeful joy (vv. 41–43).

To understand the resurrection, we must comprehend that Jesus wanted to establish the empirical evidence possible when numerous, credible eyewitnesses of a single event can corroborate one another's accounts. They used the sensory perceptions of sight, hearing, and touch to be convinced beyond all doubt that what they saw was real: Jesus had risen from the dead!

Their reliability would be questioned but never disproved, in spite of the threats that dogged them. They had previously been afraid (John 20:19), but after the resurrection they went on to boldly proclaim the gospel around the Roman Empire. The change in them, as well as the resulting existence and courage of the early church they led, is further evidence that what they saw was conclusive enough to convince them all. Even when they were later threatened with imprisonment, physical harm, and death, they tenaciously clung to their claim that Jesus died and rose again (Acts 4:13–20).

Each of them died for their testimony and refused to recant. Who does that? Only those who are convinced of their claim stick to their story if they are threatened, and their story was more than merely believing in His teaching. Their confession was that they saw Jesus raised from the dead. Some religious fanatics are willing to sacrifice themselves for a philosophy, but the apostles who changed the world were not representing a new philosophy. They were eyewitnesses to a miraculous resurrection! That important distinction separates the gospel of Jesus Christ from mere religious adherence. The apostles of Jesus and numerous others were not first and foremost convinced by religious dogma. They were persuaded because they saw Jesus alive again after His death. The power of the gospel today rests on the same truth: Jesus is still alive.

Alive and Ready to Go
Luke 24:44–49

Before the disciples had fully adjusted to the miracle of His resurrection, Jesus was already enlisting them for a new mission. They had previously accompanied Him on His teaching and preaching tours and had even been sent out on their own for brief ministry ventures (Luke 10:1–11), but what He had in mind for them next was more aggressive than anything they could have ever imagined. In fact, He was sending them on a mission larger and more expansive than any He Himself had ever attempted. They would take the message of His life, death, and resurrection to the entire world (Matt. 28:18–20; Acts 1:8)!

What would they need for that kind of undertaking? Where would they start? They had no mass communication tools. It took weeks for a letter to arrive overland by foot and potentially longer by sea. They had no significant financial resources. Their leader had died as an outlaw, hated by the religious establishment and condemned by the political powers of the empire. Their numbers were small. But they had something that made their relative limitations only mildly problematic. They had a risen Savior!

Once back from the dead, Jesus wanted to clarify the essential message they were to advocate. He turned their attention to the Scriptures of the Old Testament and started a teaching process that would crystalize the overarching theme of their Bible in a way they had never fully appreciated. He reinterpreted all of it to point to Himself. Previously we might assume the average Jewish person saw the message of the Old Testament with God's promise to the Jewish people as the main thrust. God was the hero, and Israel was the beneficiary of His blessings and plans. It's easy to see how they might have interpreted the message of their Bibles in the same way. Jesus, however, pointed them beyond territorial limitations, beyond provincial prejudices, and beyond conventional ideologies.

The message of Jesus was shaped around a foundational truth, which He revealed to them from the scrolls of their existing Bible. He claimed it was not in conflict with what He had taught them during the previous three years (v. 44). In order to help them grasp the message and have a structure in place to know how to interpret texts in the future, He "opened their minds to understand the Scriptures" (v. 45). The Greek word translated "opened" usually refers to something previously closed that had never been open, and it tends to refer to something opened thoroughly because it comes from a construction of two Greek words meaning to "open through." In other words, to open all the way. The tense of the verb suggests that once opened, the action was complete and would not need to be repeated. The disciples would never view the Scripture the same way again.

The Message
Luke 24:45–48

Since Jesus was turning the ministry He had started over to the disciples with an admonition to carry it to the world, it was necessary to clarify the message. Jesus focused on a simple formula. The core message, which the disciples and the church were to teach and preach, is a message with Jesus at the center.

The remarkable boldness of the claim about His message is found in His unflinching assertion that the Old Testament Scriptures point to Him as their essential theme and thrust (v. 44). The phrase "everything written about me in the Law of Moses and the Prophets and the Psalms" (v. 44) was the common Hebrew way of describing the entire Old Testament. All thirty-nine books of our Old Testament today (while in a different sequence and with some books combined as one in the Hebrew versions which we divide into two in English) provide the scriptural authority for the teaching of the church. The New Testament, which the earliest apostles and their close associates would write under the inspiration of the Holy Spirit (John 14:26; 2 Pet. 1:16–21), is the complete revelation of Jesus' ministry and work, as explained by the apostles from their unique understanding of the Old Testament. If Jesus were anyone less than God, this claim that the Old Testament is about Him would be more than laughable; it would be insane. Yet, standing fully alive in the presence of the men who saw Him die, gave Him an authority to make plain what He had said in more subtle ways from the beginning of His public ministry.

The gospel message Jesus sent His apostles to proclaim includes the teaching about the cross, the resurrection, and repentance and the forgiveness of sin. In addition, the essential message about Jesus is to be continually taken to the entire world (vv. 46–47).

The Power to Go
Luke 24:48–49

How did a handful of fishermen, tax collectors, and others take the message of Jesus to the entire Roman Empire in a single generation? How did they manage to "turn the world upside down" (Acts 17:6)?

We might conclude that if any group was ready to spring into action it would be the followers of Jesus present that day. After all, they had known Jesus personally and were eyewitnesses to His miracles and His conquest over death. They had a story to tell! Jesus, however, said they were to stop before they were to go (v. 49). Why? What else did they need?

Jesus advised them all to "stay in the city" (v. 49). The Greek word translated "stay" literally can mean "cease all motion." They were not yet ready to go. They needed something else, something that would make them virtually unstoppable. It must have been extremely difficult to obey that command. We could easily believe that with the message they had, many of them could barely wait to tell everyone they knew. But Jesus had a much bigger plan in mind for them. He wanted them to receive power from heaven.

Jesus referred to the Holy Spirit as "the promise of my Father," who would come to empower the disciples. That promise was fulfilled in Jerusalem fifty days after the crucifixion on an important Jewish festival, the Day of Pentecost (Acts 2:1–4). A review of the first two chapters of the book of Acts reveals how the disciples interpreted Jesus' words about "staying" in the city. They prayed in a continuous prayer meeting in the temple and in "the upper room," presumably in a private residence (Luke 24:53; Acts 1:13–14).

Jesus described the experience with the Holy Spirit as being "clothed with power from on high" (Luke 24:49). The Greek word translated "clothed" is the word from which we get our word "to endue." They were to be "endued" with the Spirit. The word comes into English from Greek through Latin, where it means "to put on clothes." The church, empowered by the Holy Spirit, is pictured here wrapped in the Spirit as if wearing Him like a garment. We are to be covered by the Holy Spirit like a person is covered with clothing. This picturesque way of describing the presence of the Spirit is only one of a variety of ways the New Testament portrays the Spirit's role in the believer's life (Luke 3:16; Acts 1:8; Acts 2:4; Eph. 5:18).

When the New Testament writers communicate the experience of the Holy Spirit's activity in the followers of Jesus, the result is always the same—power! Our word *dynamic* comes from the Greek word here translated "power." The Holy Spirit is the dynamic power of God that made all the difference in finally preparing the disciples to preach and teach in Jesus' name. Jesus said the source of the power of the Spirit is "from on high" (Luke 24:49). The phrase in Greek could be literally translated "out of the highest heaven" (author's translation). The Holy Spirit is the gift to the believer from the throne of God Himself. No wonder the early church was so successful in fulfilling their mission. They were empowered by the Holy Spirit from God.

Now

The principles and promises that guided the early church have never been retracted or changed. Nowhere in Scripture do we learn that believers today are to do less or depend on less than that which was expected of the original disciples. We have the marching orders of Jesus to take the message to our world (Matt. 28:18–20) just as they did. We are left with the contours of His message—the death and resurrection of Christ, repentance, and the forgiveness of sins. Fortunately we also still have access to the power of the Holy Spirit who gives our preaching, teaching, and ministry the stamp of God's authority.

The life of Jesus of Nazareth was like no other life ever lived. Through His Spirit and His church He continues to work in our lives and in our world today. He is presented in the New Testament as the incarnation of God. He is revealed as fully man and fully God.

After years of considering the claims about Jesus, I am a convinced believer. I believe what the Bible says about Him is true. I believe His death on the cross paid the penalty for my sin. I believe He rose from the dead. I believe He is the Messiah who was predicted by the Old Testament prophets. I believe He is fully God. I believe He is coming again. I am a follower of Jesus of Nazareth, and I know Him as both Savior and Lord.

What do you believe? What do you think about Jesus? Who do you say Jesus is?

For Memory and Meditation

"And he said to them, 'Thus it is written, that the Christ should suffer and on the third day rise from the dead.'" Luke 24:46

---

[1] Ben Golliver, "Ex-NBA player Quinton Ross: erroneous death report made for 'tough day,'" nba.si.com/2014/03/25/quinton-ross-false-report-death-nba-player, accessed March 19, 2014.

Epilogue
Knowing Jesus Personally

Are you a follower of Jesus? Many who read this book are, but perhaps you are not, or maybe you're not certain. The following brief paragraphs will explain from a biblical perspective how you can begin a relationship with the greatest person who ever lived, Jesus of Nazareth.

One night Jesus was approached privately by a religious leader who was asking questions about the Lord's teaching. The religious leader had never heard anything quite like what Jesus had to say. As a result, he was unclear about what it meant or if it was true. From that conversation came some of the most familiar words Jesus ever spoke. What Jesus told the religious man that night can assist you, too, with the questions you may have.

Jesus told the man that it isn't enough to be religious. Nicodemus, the man who came to Jesus, was an educated religious leader, but Jesus said to him, "You must be born again" (John 3:7). In other words, following Christ and being His disciple involves a spiritual rebirth that is a gift from God. Jesus went on to remind Nicodemus that man is a sinner and prefers to live in spiritual darkness, where he believes his life will not be held accountable. Jesus said it this way, "And this is the judgment: the light has come into the world, and people loved the darkness rather than the light because their works were evil. For everyone who does wicked things hates the light and does not come to the light, lest his works should be exposed" (John 3:19–20).

Obviously Jesus does not want to leave anyone in a sinful condition separated from God, so He did something extraordinary. On the cross Jesus Himself took the penalty for sin. The Bible says, "For while we were still weak, at the right time Christ died for the ungodly. For one will scarcely die for a righteous person—though perhaps for a good person one would dare even to die—but God shows his love for us in that while we were still sinners, Christ died for us" (Rom. 5:6–8).

Have you ever committed a sin? The Bible says Jesus died for sin—not for His own but for yours and mine. Why would Jesus go to such an extreme length to forgive sin? Why did He have to die? Obviously God looks at our sin differently than we do. We learn to excuse sin because we are guilty of some sin, and we live with other people who also sin every day. After a while we realize that if we are going to get along with people we cannot do it very well if we are constantly critical and judgmental. But God views sin from a different perspective because He is not sinful. He has never sinned. Even Jesus never committed a sin (Heb. 4:15). You, no doubt, know someone who is far worse than you are, but God views all of us as broken by sin, regardless of how willing we are to compare ourselves to someone who appears to us to be far worse. The Bible says, "For all have sinned and fall short of the glory of God" (Rom. 3:23). There are no exceptions.

The problem with sin is that it carries a penalty. Like any broken law there is a price to pay for those found guilty. God's judgment against sin is permanent. The Bible says, "For the wages of sin is death, but the free gift of God is eternal life in Christ Jesus our Lord" (Rom. 6:23). Death is the penalty for sin. The Bible speaks of death in at least three ways. Of course there is physical death. Next there is eternal death in the place called hell. Finally, there is the reality of being dead spiritually until Christ comes to live within us and give us life. Sin leads to death, which in all of its terrible expressions is separation from God. That's why Jesus had to die. It was the only way to pay for our sin.

But the gospel is "good news"! The Bible says, "The free gift of God is eternal life in Christ Jesus our Lord" (Rom. 6:23b). You can receive God's gift of forgiveness and eternal life right now! What does that involve? The Bible promises when we receive Christ all of our sins will be forgiven, we will be assured of going to heaven when we die, and we will be in a new relationship with God through our faith in Christ, which begins immediately and never ends. Would you like to receive this gift of eternal life in Christ?

In order to become a follower of Jesus and receive God's gift of eternal life, we turn away from our sin and place our faith in Jesus Christ for salvation. By doing so, we are admitting His death on the cross is the only way for us to be saved, and we are turning our back on any hope of getting to heaven in any other way. The Bible says, "And there is salvation in no one else, for there is no other name under heaven given among men by which we must be saved" (Acts 4:12).

How do we receive God's gift of forgiveness and eternal life? We must acknowledge and repent of our sin. The Bible says, "Repent therefore, and turn back, that your sins may be blotted out" (Acts 3:19). Repentance means to turn and go in a different direction. It means we are sorry for our sins and we are willing for God's power to change us from the inside out.

In addition to repenting of sin, we must place our faith in Christ. Remember the conversation Jesus had with Nicodemus, the religious leader? In what may be the most famous verse of Scripture in the New Testament, Jesus said, "For God so loved the world, that he gave his only Son, that whoever believes in him should not perish but have eternal life" (John 3:16). Will you place your faith in Jesus right now? How? The Bible says faith is expressed from the heart by calling upon the name of the Lord Jesus. The Bible says, "If you confess with your mouth that Jesus is Lord and believe in your heart that God raised him from the dead, you will be saved" (Rom. 10:9). That is God's promise and you can believe it!

If you would like to become a follower of Jesus and receive the gift of eternal life promised by God, perhaps a prayer like the following will help you express your need to Him. "Dear God, I know I have sinned against You. Please forgive me. Lord Jesus, I believe You died on the cross for me, and I invite You to come into my life right now and save me." If you have called on the name of the Lord for salvation, you have done the right thing! I encourage you to contact a Christian friend or a local church or pastor right away to let them know. They can help you get started living the Christian life. You can even contact me. I will be glad to help you as you begin the life of a fully devoted follower of Jesus!

God bless you.

J. Kie Bowman
Austin, Texas